# YOUR CHINESE
# HOROSCOPE 1996

## ABOUT THE AUTHOR

Neil Somerville is one of the leading writers in the West on Chinese horoscopes. He has been interested in Eastern forms of divination for many years and believes that much can be learned from the ancient wisdom of the East. His annual book on Chinese horoscopes has built up an international following and *Your Chinese Horoscope 1996* marks the ninth year of publication. He is also the author of *Chinese Love Signs* (Thorsons, 1995).

Neil Somerville was born in the year of the Water Snake. His wife was born under the sign of the Monkey, his son is an Ox and daughter a Horse.

# YOUR CHINESE HOROSCOPE 1996

NEIL SOMERVILLE

*What the Year of the Rat holds in store for you*

**Thorsons**
*An Imprint of* HarperCollins*Publishers*

TO ROS, RICHARD AND EMILY.

Thorsons
An Imprint of HarperCollins*Publishers*
77–85 Fulham Palace Road
Hammersmith, London W6 8JB
1160 Battery Street
San Francisco, California 94111–1213

Published by Thorsons 1995

10 9 8 7 6 5 4 3 2

A catalogue record for this book
is available from the British Library

ISBN 1 85538 450 7

Printed in Great Britain by
HarperCollinsManufacturing Glasgow

Illustrations by Josephine Sumner

# CONTENTS

—◆◆◆—

# ACKNOWLEDGEMENTS

In writing *Your Chinese Horoscope 1996* I am grateful for the assistance and support that those around me have given. I wish to acknowledge Theodora Lau's *The Handbook of Chinese Horoscopes* (Harper & Row, 1979; Arrow, 1981), which was particularly useful to me in my research.

In addition to Ms Lau's work, I commend the following books to those who wish to find out more about Chinese horoscopes: Catherine Aubier, *Chinese Zodiac Signs* (Arrow, 1984), series of 12 books; Paula Delsol, *Chinese Horoscopes* (Pan, 1973); E. A. Crawford and Teresa Kennedy, *Chinese Elemental Astrology* (Piatkus, 1992); Barry Fantoni, *Barry Fantoni's Chinese Horoscopes* (Warner, 1994); Jean-Michel Huon de Kermadec, *The Way to Chinese Astrology* (Unwin, 1983); Kwok Man-Ho, *Authentic Chinese Horoscopes* (Arrow, 1987), series of 12 books; Paul Rigby and Harvey Bean, *Chinese Astrologics* (Publications Division, South China Morning Post Ltd., 1981), Derek Walters, *Ming Shu* (Pagoda Books, 1987) and *The Chinese Astrology Workbook* (The Aquarian Press, 1988), Suzanne White, *Suzanne White Book of Chinese Chance* (Fontana/Collins, 1976) and *The New Astrology* (Pan, 1987) and *The New Chinese Astrology* (Pan, 1994).

# INTRODUCTION

———•◆•———

The origins of Chinese horoscopes have been lost in the mists of time. It is known that oriental astrologers practised their art many thousands of years ago and, even today, Chinese astrology continues to fascinate and intrigue.

In Chinese astrology there are 12 signs named after 12 different animals. No one quite knows how the signs acquired their names, but there is one legend that offers an explanation.

According to this legend, one Chinese New Year, the Buddha invited all the animals in his kingdom to come before him. Unfortunately – for reasons best known to the animals – only 12 turned up. The first to arrive was the Rat, followed by the Ox, Tiger, Rabbit, Dragon, Snake, Horse, Goat, Monkey, Rooster, Dog and finally the Pig.

In gratitude, the Buddha decided to name a year after each of the animals and those born during that year would inherit some of the personality of that animal. Therefore those born in the year of the Ox would be hard-working, resolute and stubborn – just like the Ox – while those born in the year of the Dog would be loyal and faithful – just like the Dog.

While not everyone can possibly share all the characteristics of a sign, it is incredible what similarities do occur and this is partly where the fascination of Chinese horoscopes lies.

In addition to the 12 signs of the Chinese zodiac there are also five elements and these have a strengthening or moderating influence upon the sign. Details about the effects of the elements are given in each of the chapters on the 12 signs.

To find out which sign you were born under, refer to the tables on pages ix–xii. As the Chinese year is based on the lunar year and does not start until late January or early February, it is particularly important for anyone born in those two months to check carefully the dates of the Chinese year in which they were born.

Also included, in the Appendix, are two charts showing the compatibility between the signs for both personal and business relationships, and details about the signs ruling the different hours of the day. From this it is possible to locate your ascendant and, as in Western astrology, this has a significant influence on your personality.

In writing this book, I have taken the unusual step of combining the intriguing nature of Chinese horoscopes with the Western desire to know what the future holds and have based my interpretations upon various factors relating to each of the signs. This is the ninth year in which *Your Chinese Horoscope* has been published and I am pleased that so many have found the sections on the forthcoming year of benefit and that the advice has been constructive and helpful. Remember, though, that at all times you are the master of your own destiny. I sincerely hope that *Your Chinese Horoscope 1996* will prove interesting and helpful for the year ahead.

# THE CHINESE YEARS

| | | | | | |
|---|---|---|---|---|---|
| Rat | 31 January | 1900 | to | 18 February | 1901 |
| Ox | 19 February | 1901 | to | 7 February | 1902 |
| Tiger | 8 February | 1902 | to | 28 January | 1903 |
| Rabbit | 29 January | 1903 | to | 15 February | 1904 |
| Dragon | 16 February | 1904 | to | 3 February | 1905 |
| Snake | 4 February | 1905 | to | 24 January | 1906 |
| Horse | 25 January | 1906 | to | 12 February | 1907 |
| Goat | 13 February | 1907 | to | 1 February | 1908 |
| Monkey | 2 February | 1908 | to | 21 January | 1909 |
| Rooster | 22 January | 1909 | to | 9 February | 1910 |
| Dog | 10 February | 1910 | to | 29 January | 1911 |
| Pig | 30 January | 1911 | to | 17 February | 1912 |
| Rat | 18 February | 1912 | to | 5 February | 1913 |
| Ox | 6 February | 1913 | to | 24 January | 1914 |
| Tiger | 25 January | 1914 | to | 13 February | 1915 |
| Rabbit | 14 February | 1915 | to | 2 February | 1916 |
| Dragon | 3 February | 1916 | to | 22 January | 1917 |
| Snake | 23 January | 1917 | to | 10 February | 1918 |
| Horse | 11 February | 1918 | to | 31 January | 1919 |
| Goat | 1 February | 1919 | to | 19 February | 1920 |
| Monkey | 20 February | 1920 | to | 7 February | 1921 |
| Rooster | 8 February | 1921 | to | 27 January | 1922 |
| Dog | 28 January | 1922 | to | 15 February | 1923 |
| Pig | 16 February | 1923 | to | 4 February | 1924 |

| | | | | | | |
|---|---|---|---|---|---|---|
| Rat | 5 | February | 1924 | to | 24 January | 1925 |
| Ox | 25 | January | 1925 | to | 12 February | 1926 |
| Tiger | 13 | February | 1926 | to | 1 February | 1927 |
| Rabbit | 2 | February | 1927 | to | 22 January | 1928 |
| Dragon | 23 | January | 1928 | to | 9 February | 1929 |
| Snake | 10 | February | 1929 | to | 29 January | 1930 |
| Horse | 30 | January | 1930 | to | 16 February | 1931 |
| Goat | 17 | February | 1931 | to | 5 February | 1932 |
| Monkey | 6 | February | 1932 | to | 25 January | 1933 |
| Rooster | 26 | January | 1933 | to | 13 February | 1934 |
| Dog | 14 | February | 1934 | to | 3 February | 1935 |
| Pig | 4 | February | 1935 | to | 23 January | 1936 |
| Rat | 24 | January | 1936 | to | 10 February | 1937 |
| Ox | 11 | February | 1937 | to | 30 January | 1938 |
| Tiger | 31 | January | 1938 | to | 18 February | 1939 |
| Rabbit | 19 | February | 1939 | to | 7 February | 1940 |
| Dragon | 8 | February | 1940 | to | 26 January | 1941 |
| Snake | 27 | January | 1941 | to | 14 February | 1942 |
| Horse | 15 | February | 1942 | to | 4 February | 1943 |
| Goat | 5 | February | 1943 | to | 24 January | 1944 |
| Monkey | 25 | January | 1944 | to | 12 February | 1945 |
| Rooster | 13 | February | 1945 | to | 1 February | 1946 |
| Dog | 2 | February | 1946 | to | 21 January | 1947 |
| Pig | 22 | January | 1947 | to | 9 February | 1948 |
| Rat | 10 | February | 1948 | to | 28 January | 1949 |
| Ox | 29 | January | 1949 | to | 16 February | 1950 |
| Tiger | 17 | February | 1950 | to | 5 February | 1951 |
| Rabbit | 6 | February | 1951 | to | 26 January | 1952 |
| Dragon | 27 | January | 1952 | to | 13 February | 1953 |
| Snake | 14 | February | 1953 | to | 2 February | 1954 |
| Horse | 3 | February | 1954 | to | 23 January | 1955 |

| Goat | 24 January | 1955 | to | 11 February | 1956 |
|------|------------|------|----|-----------|------|
| Monkey | 12 February | 1956 | to | 30 January | 1957 |
| Rooster | 31 January | 1957 | to | 17 February | 1958 |
| Dog | 18 February | 1958 | to | 7 February | 1959 |
| Pig | 8 February | 1959 | to | 27 January | 1960 |
| Rat | 28 January | 1960 | to | 14 February | 1961 |
| Ox | 15 February | 1961 | to | 4 February | 1962 |
| Tiger | 5 February | 1962 | to | 24 January | 1963 |
| Rabbit | 25 January | 1963 | to | 12 February | 1964 |
| Dragon | 13 February | 1964 | to | 1 February | 1965 |
| Snake | 2 February | 1965 | to | 20 January | 1966 |
| Horse | 21 January | 1966 | to | 8 February | 1967 |
| Goat | 9 February | 1967 | to | 29 January | 1968 |
| Monkey | 30 January | 1968 | to | 16 February | 1969 |
| Rooster | 17 February | 1969 | to | 5 February | 1970 |
| Dog | 6 February | 1970 | to | 26 January | 1971 |
| Pig | 27 January | 1971 | to | 14 February | 1972 |
| Rat | 15 February | 1972 | to | 2 February | 1973 |
| Ox | 3 February | 1973 | to | 22 January | 1974 |
| Tiger | 23 January | 1974 | to | 10 February | 1975 |
| Rabbit | 11 February | 1975 | to | 30 January | 1976 |
| Dragon | 31 January | 1976 | to | 17 February | 1977 |
| Snake | 18 February | 1977 | to | 6 February | 1978 |
| Horse | 7 February | 1978 | to | 27 January | 1979 |
| Goat | 28 January | 1979 | to | 15 February | 1980 |
| Monkey | 16 February | 1980 | to | 4 February | 1981 |
| Rooster | 5 February | 1981 | to | 24 January | 1982 |
| Dog | 25 January | 1982 | to | 12 February | 1983 |
| Pig | 13 February | 1983 | to | 1 February | 1984 |
| Rat | 2 February | 1984 | to | 19 February | 1985 |
| Ox | 20 February | 1985 | to | 8 February | 1986 |

| Tiger | 9 February | 1986 | to | 28 January | 1987 |
|---|---|---|---|---|---|
| Rabbit | 29 January | 1987 | to | 16 February | 1988 |
| Dragon | 17 February | 1988 | to | 5 February | 1989 |
| Snake | 6 February | 1989 | to | 26 January | 1990 |
| Horse | 27 January | 1990 | to | 14 February | 1991 |
| Goat | 15 February | 1991 | to | 3 February | 1992 |
| Monkey | 4 February | 1992 | to | 22 January | 1993 |
| Rooster | 23 January | 1993 | to | 9 February | 1994 |
| Dog | 10 February | 1994 | to | 30 January | 1995 |
| Pig | 31 January | 1995 | to | 18 February | 1996 |
| Rat | 19 February | 1996 | to | 6 February | 1997 |

*Note:* The names of the signs in the Chinese zodiac occasionally differ in the various books on Chinese astrology, although the characteristics of the signs remain the same. In some books the Ox is referred to as the Buffalo or Bull, the Rabbit as the Hare or Cat, the Goat as the Sheep and the Pig as the Boar.

For the sake of convenience, the male gender is used throughout this book. Unless otherwise stated, the characteristics of the signs apply to both sexes.

Be resolved and the thing is done.
*Chinese proverb.*

# WELCOME TO
# THE YEAR OF THE RAT

Whether raiding rubbish heaps or foraging elsewhere for scraps, the Rat is a supreme opportunist. He is also strong-willed and determined to make the most of any situation in which he finds himself. This spirit of resourcefulness will become very evident in 1996, the Year of the Rat.

The Rat year marks the start of a new 12-year cycle of Chinese years and in many respects Rat years are charac-terized by change, both political and social. They are also considered years of opportunity and this will be reflected by a significant upturn in the economies of many countries throughout the world. Levels of industrial output will be up and many industries will finally pull out of the reces-sion that has dogged their progress in recent years. Unemployment, as a consequence, will fall and there is likely to be more mobility in the labour market than has been seen in recent years.

Two areas which have already seen tremendous growth are the home entertainment industry and telecommunica-tions, and both areas will continue to show strong growth in the Rat year. More cable and satellite services will be on offer and services such as shopping by television – which already exists in some countries – will become more wide-spread. With the amazing technological advances that have taken place, it all seems a long way from the time when, just 60 years ago and in another Rat year, the millionth telephone was installed in the London area!

With a general air of optimism prevailing, consumer spending will be very much up on recent years and this in turn will reflect favourably in the financial sector and on stock markets around the world. However, while economically things may appear good, it would still be a wise move for those who are able to make savings for less prosperous years. As history has so often shown, boom conditions do not last forever!

Politically, Rat years can be very active and many countries, including the United States, will hold elections in 1996. In some cases established leaders will be replaced by younger and more innovative politicians, swept to power on waves of enthusiasm and promises of greater prosperity. In particular, there could be significant changes in Russia and some of the new countries in Eastern Europe. Some Commonwealth countries, too, notably Canada and Australia, will see several important political developments over the year.

In the United States the election promises to be close. The primaries will be fiercely contested and will offer some surprises in the choice of possible contenders for the Presidential election. However, the present President, Bill Clinton, is born under the sign of the Dog and it should be noted that Dogs generally fare well in Rat years.

Another feature of 1996 could be startling revelations about people in the public eye. Some of these could have major political consequences. It was in a Rat year that burglars were caught in the Watergate hotel – events that led to the resignation of President Nixon. In 1996 the media will be active – and in some cases ruthless – in their investigations and pursuit of stories.

The spotlight is also rarely off Royal Families and 1996 will be no exception. Indeed, previous Rat years have been significant for Royalty – it was in a Rat year when the abdication crisis occurred in Britain and Edward VIII abdicated in favour of George VI, and when, in a later Rat year, Queen Wilhemina of the Netherlands abdicated in favour of Queen Juliana. In 1996 several Royal Families will again see important changes take place and in Britain some of these could have a bearing on the role of the monarchy in future years.

Although, as in all years, there will be some harrowing events, Rat years are generally years of hope, optimism and enjoyment. People will generally enjoy themselves and many will have more time available for leisure activities. In addition to the continuing growth in home entertainment, many will take the opportunity to travel, take part in sporting and outdoor activities or just go out and have fun. Many previous Rat years have indeed been characterized by this element of leisure, enjoyment and entertainment – it was, for example, in a Rat year when the first of the famous Butlin holiday camps opened in Britain and when the BBC began the world's first regular television service. Also, 1996 is the year of the Olympics and not only will these provide excitement and enjoyment for millions but they could also inspire some to engage in more sporting and outdoor activities. It is certainly possible that a new fitness craze will emerge over the year.

Rat years also favour the arts and 1996 will be no exception. Some major works of literature are likely to appear over the year – *The Tale of Peter Rabbit* by Beatrix Potter and *A Passage to India* by E. M. Forster are just two of the many famous books that first appeared in Rat years – and there will also be many box-office successes both in the cinema and theatre. One other feature of 1996 could be the growth in popularity of books of a poetic and philosophic nature.

Generally, there will be good reason for most to enjoy the Year of the Rat. There will be a sense of growth and optimism to the year and many will see an improvement in their lifestyle and, quite possibly, financial improvement as well. Almost all signs can benefit in some way from the Rat year and with so much opportunity about many will do well in 1996 and enjoy the year. This is very much a year of activity and progress and I sincerely hope that you will do well over the year and realize many of your hopes and desires.

---

31 JANUARY 1900 ～ 18 FEBRUARY 1901          *Metal Rat*

18 FEBRUARY 1912 ～ 5 FEBRUARY 1913          *Water Rat*

5 FEBRUARY 1924 ～ 24 JANUARY 1925          *Wood Rat*

24 JANUARY 1936 ～ 10 FEBRUARY 1937          *Fire Rat*

10 FEBRUARY 1948 ～ 28 JANUARY 1949          *Earth Rat*

28 JANUARY 1960 ～ 14 FEBRUARY 1961          *Metal Rat*

15 FEBRUARY 1972 ～ 2 FEBRUARY 1973          *Water Rat*

2 FEBRUARY 1984 ～ 19 FEBRUARY 1985          *Wood Rat*

19 FEBRUARY 1996 ～ 6 FEBRUARY 1997          *Fire Rat*

---

# THE
# RAT

# THE PERSONALITY OF THE RAT

Every individual has a place to fill in the world and is important in some respect whether he chooses to be so or not.

– *Nathaniel Hawthorne: a Rat*

The Rat is born under the sign of charm. He is intelligent, popular, and loves attending parties and large social gatherings. He is able to establish friendships with remarkable ease and people generally feel relaxed in his company. He is a very social creature and is genuinely interested in the welfare and activities of others. He has a good understanding of human nature and his advice and opinions are often sought.

The Rat is a hard and diligent worker. He is also very imaginative and is never short of ideas. However, he does sometimes lack the confidence to promote his ideas as much as he should and this can often prevent him from securing the recognition and credit he so often deserves.

The Rat is very observant and many Rats have made excellent writers and journalists. The Rat also excels at personnel and PR work and any job which brings him into contact with people and the media. His skills are particularly appreciated in times of crisis, for the Rat has an incredibly strong sense of self-preservation. When it comes to finding a way out of an awkward situation, he is certain to be the one who comes up with a solution.

The Rat loves to be where there is a lot of action, but should he ever find himself in a very bureaucratic or restrictive environment he can become a stickler for discipline and routine.

He is also something of an opportunist and is constantly on the look-out for ways in which he can improve his wealth and lifestyle. He rarely lets an opportunity go by and can become involved in so many plans and schemes that he sometimes squanders his energies and achieves very little as a result. He is also rather gullible and can be taken in by those less scrupulous than himself.

Another characteristic of the Rat is his attitude to money. He is very thrifty and to some he may appear a little mean. The reason for this is purely that he likes to keep his money within his family. He can be most generous to his partner, his children and close friends and relatives. He can also be generous to himself, for he often finds it impossible to deprive himself of any luxury or object he fancies. The Rat is also very acquisitive and can be a notorious hoarder. He hates waste and is rarely prepared to throw anything away. He can also be rather greedy and will rarely refuse an invitation for a free meal or a complimentary ticket to some lavish function.

The Rat is a good conversationalist, although he can occasionally be a little indiscreet. He can be highly critical of others – for an honest and unbiased opinion, the Rat is a superb critic – and sometimes will use confidential information to his own advantage. However, as the Rat has such a bright and irresistible nature, most are prepared to forgive him for his slight indiscretions.

Throughout his long and eventful life, the Rat will make many friends and will find that he is especially well-suited to those born under his own sign and those of the Ox, Dragon and Monkey. The Rat can also get on well with those born under the signs of the Tiger, Snake, Rooster,

Dog and Pig, but the rather sensitive Rabbit and Goat will find the Rat a little too critical and blunt for their liking. The Horse and Rat will also find it difficult to get on with each other – the Rat craves security and will find the Horse's changeable moods and rather independent nature a little unsettling.

The Rat is very family orientated and will do anything to please his nearest and dearest. He is exceptionally loyal to his parents and can himself be a very caring and loving parent. He will take an interest in all his children's activities and will see that they want for nothing. The Rat usually has a large family.

The female Rat has a kindly, outgoing nature and involves herself in a multitude of different activities. She is a superb hostess and will usually have a wide circle of very good friends. She is conscientious about the upkeep of her home and has superb taste in home furnishings. She is extremely supportive to the other members of her family and, due to her resourceful, friendly and persevering nature, can do well in practically any career she enters.

Although the Rat is essentially outgoing and something of an extrovert, he is also a very private individual. He tends to keep his feelings to himself and, while he is not averse to learning what other people are doing, he resents anyone prying too closely into his own affairs. He also does not like solitude and if he is alone for any length of time he can easily get depressed.

The Rat is undoubtedly very talented, but more often than not he fails to capitalize on his many abilities. He has a tendency to become involved in too many schemes and chase after too many opportunities all at one time. If he were to slow down and concentrate on one thing at a time he could become very successful. If not, success and wealth could elude him. But the Rat, with his tremendous ability to charm, will rarely, if ever, be without friends.

# THE FIVE DIFFERENT TYPES OF RAT

In addition to the 12 signs of the Chinese zodiac, there are five elements and these have a strengthening or moderating influence on the sign. The effects of the five elements on the Rat are described below, together with the years in which the elements were exercising their influence. Therefore all Rats born in 1900 and 1960 are Metal Rats, those born in 1912 and 1972 are Water Rats, and so on.

## *Metal Rat: 1900, 1960*
This Rat has excellent taste and certainly knows how to appreciate the finer things in life. His home is comfortable and nicely decorated and he is forever entertaining or mixing in fashionable circles. He has considerable financial acumen and invests his money well. On the surface the Metal Rat appears cheerful and confident, but deep down he can be troubled by worries that are quite often of his own making. He is exceptionally loyal to his family and friends.

## Water Rat: 1912, 1972

The Water Rat is intelligent and very astute. He is a deep thinker and can express his thoughts clearly and persuasively. He is always eager to learn and is talented in many different areas. The Water Rat is usually very popular, but his fear of loneliness can sometimes lead him into mixing with the wrong sort of company. He is a particularly skilful writer, but he can get side-tracked very easily and should try to concentrate on just one thing at a time.

## Wood Rat: 1924, 1984

The Wood Rat has a friendly, outgoing personality and is most popular with his colleagues and friends. He has a quick, agile brain and likes to turn his hand to anything he thinks may be useful. His one fear is insecurity, but given his intelligence and capabilities this fear is usually unfounded. He has a good sense of humour, enjoys travel and, due to his highly imaginative nature, can be a gifted writer or artist.

## Fire Rat: 1936, 1996

The Fire Rat is rarely still and seems to have a never-ending supply of energy and enthusiasm. He loves being involved in the action – be it travel, following up new ideas or campaigning for a cause in which he fervently believes. He is an original thinker and hates being bound by petty restrictions or the dictates of others. He can be forthright in his views, but can sometimes get carried away in the excitement of the moment and commit himself to various undertakings without checking what all the implications might be. He has a resilient nature and, with the right support, can often go far in life.

## Earth Rat: 1948

This Rat is astute and very level-headed. He rarely takes unnecessary chances and, while he is constantly trying to improve his financial status, he is prepared to proceed slowly and leave nothing to chance. The Earth Rat is probably not as adventurous as the other types of Rat and prefers to remain in familiar areas rather than rush headlong into something he knows little about. He is talented, conscientious and caring towards his loved ones, but at the same time can be self-conscious and worry a little too much about the image he is trying to project.

# PROSPECTS FOR THE RAT IN 1996

The Chinese New Year starts on 19 February 1996. Until then, the old year, the Year of the Pig, is still making its presence felt.

The Year of the Pig (31 January 1995 to 18 February 1996) will have been a generally positive year for the Rat. In what remains of the Pig year, he should continue to set about his activities in a purposeful way. However, in all his activities he would do well to concentrate on specific objectives rather than spread his energies too widely or commit himself to too much. He can accomplish a considerable amount in the period from September 1995 to January

1996, but his efforts must be directed towards specific purposes.

In his work the Rat can look forward to making satisfactory gains and his ideas, enthusiasm and conscientiousness will impress those in authority. The Rat year will be an especially positive year for him and anything constructive that he can do in the closing stages of the Pig year will be very much to his advantage. If he can widen his experience and skills at this time he will find that this will do much to enhance his prospects. Similarly, those Rats seeking work should remain vigilant for opportunities to pursue or ways in which they can extend their skills. As the new year approaches, the Rat would do well to give some thought to his hopes and plans for the year ahead. Thus prepared, he will be better able to take advantage of the exciting prospects that await him in his own year.

The Rat would also do well to use the latter part of the Pig year to deal with any outstanding matters, particularly unanswered correspondence or unfinished jobs around the house. With a determined effort he will be delighted with what he is able to accomplish.

Domestically and socially, the closing months of the Pig year will be a busy and splendid time for him and he can look forward to some most enjoyable occasions with his family and friends.

The Year of the Rat starts on 19 February and is going to be a significant and enriching year for the Rat. From almost the very start of the year he will feel more confident and more determined than ever to make the most of himself and his many abilities.

By adopting and maintaining a positive stance, the Rat

can turn 1996 into one of the most rewarding years he has enjoyed for a long time. Almost all his activities will go well and bring him pleasure but, in order to capitalize on the favourable trends that prevail, he should decide on his priorities and resist the temptation to get involved in too many activities all at the same time.

The Rat's work is most favourably aspected and it is an ideal time for him to seek promotion or transfer to a new and more challenging position; it is also a year in which he can confidently advance new ideas and start new projects. The Rat is adept at spotting opportunities and there will be many times over the year when he can put his skills to good use and further his interests. Throughout 1996 he should remain alert to all that is going on around him and follow up the openings that he sees. Almost all Rats will make significant progress in their work over the year and the months of March, April and October could be particularly significant for career opportunities.

Many Rats seeking work will also enjoy good fortune and their persistence and determination will be rewarded – quite often at a time when they least expect it. Again, they should remain alert for opportunities to pursue but also look at types of work which they may not have fully considered before. A completely different type of work could prove a stimulating challenge for them as well as opening up opportunities that might not have been available before.

The Rat will enjoy a considerable improvement in his financial situation over the year and a savings scheme he starts or investment that he makes could prove most successful. However, while the Rat will enjoy considerable good fortune in money matters, he should remain his usual thrifty and prudent self. The upturn he will enjoy in 1996 will not last forever and he will, in future years, be grateful for any savings he is able to make now.

The Rat's domestic life will be generally busy over the year and will bring him considerable pleasure. He will take much pride in the achievements of a close relation and any additional support he feels able to give will be thoroughly appreciated. Many Rats will also have good reason for a family celebration over the year – either because they have fulfilled a personal ambition or because they have some splendid personal news. This could include an engagement or wedding or the birth of a child or grandchild.

Those around the Rat will be most supportive over the year and will give him much useful advice and encouragement. If there is any matter concerning him or if he is in a dilemma over a decision, he should not hesitate to discuss his concerns with others. In many cases he could find he is worrying unnecessarily and that others will be able to reassure and assist him.

The Rat will also lead a pleasurable social life in 1996 and can look forward to attending a variety of functions over the year. There will be plenty of opportunities for him to increase his circle of friends and, for the unattached Rat, this is a splendid year for romance and for getting married. Those Rats who may have been feeling lonely or who are unhappy with their present situation should make every effort to immerse themselves in new activities or perhaps join a local society or club. They will be truly glad they have made the effort.

Property matters will also figure prominently over the

year and many Rats will spend time carrying out improvements to their home or moving. In all cases the Rat will be well satisfied with the results, although the process of carrying out home projects or moving could take him longer – and be more costly – than he first envisaged. Also, when carrying out jobs around the house, the Rat does need to be particularly careful when lifting or moving heavy objects. Without care he could sprain himself and cause himself some discomfiture. Similarly, when using potentially dangerous pieces of equipment, the Rat needs to follow all the precautions necessary. Although the Rat year may be an auspicious time for him, it is not a year in which he can ignore his personal safety!

There will be several opportunities for the Rat to travel over the year – sometimes at short notice – and any holidays or breaks that he takes will prove both enjoyable and beneficial for him. He could, however, find it helpful to read up about his destination before he leaves – this way his visit will be made all the more interesting. However, if he visits a country with a widely differing climate from his own, he should make sure he goes well prepared and takes all the creams, medicines and clothing that may be needed. To ignore recommended advice could mar what will otherwise be a splendid time away.

Generally, the Rat can make pleasing gains this year in almost any area of his life. But his level of progress does rest with him. He should decide what he wants to achieve over the year – whether it is a new job, a change of accommodation or attaining a personal ambition – and should work towards that goal. The aspects are most favourable and it is up to the Rat himself to give of his best and take advantage of the considerable opportunities that his own year brings. For the bold and determined Rat, this can be a truly auspicious and rewarding year.

As far as the different types of Rat are concerned, 1996 will be a splendid year for the *Metal Rat*. Throughout the year, however, he needs to set about his activities in a purposeful and determined manner. He has many skills and he should resolve to make the most of them. He should promote his ideas, advance new projects and pursue any opportunities that he sees. With his personable manner and keen intelligence, the Metal Rat is in a good position to impress others and this will help his progress considerably. If there is some objective or ambition he wishes to attain, now is the time to act. In his work the Metal Rat will make considerable progress and many Metal Rats will obtain a new and more responsible position as the year progresses. For those who are unhappy in their present situation or who feel they have not been making the progress they would like, now is the time to take the initiative and look for other ways in which they can use their skills. The Metal Rat's ingenuity and resourcefulness will serve him well over the year and by acting positively, almost all Metal Rats will make significant progress. The Metal Rat will also enjoy a considerable improvement in his finances but, despite his usually careful way with money matters, he would still do well to keep a close watch over his sometimes indulgent nature. He could usefully put any savings he makes towards home improvements or a holiday later in the year. The Metal Rat's domestic life will give him much satisfaction and he can look forward to some most enjoyable times with his family and friends. All around him will be keen to support and encourage him and he would do well to listen to their views and to any advice they give him. They hold him in high esteem and speak with his best interests at heart. The Metal Rat may, however, need to assist someone who has an awkward matter to deal with over the year. While this may cause him some concern at the time, his considerate and attentive attitude will be greatly appreciated. The Metal Rat will obtain enjoyment from his various interests over the year, especially any that involve him in outdoor activities. Travel is well aspected and any journeys and holidays that he takes are likely to go well. Generally, this will be a most favourable year for the Metal Rat and, providing he sets about his activities in a positive and organized way, he can achieve much. With his genial nature and many talents, the Metal Rat has much in his favour. This is a year when he can make substantial progress and start to capitalize on his considerable potential.

This will be an active and favourable year for the *Water Rat*. His personal life in particular will be a great source of joy to him and many Water Rats will have good cause for a celebration over the year. This could include an engagement, marriage or birth in the family. Throughout 1996 the Water Rat can look forward to some splendid and happy times with those around him. He will also spend much time over the year dealing with property matters. Many Water Rats will change their accommodation or carry out projects around their home. In either case this will give the Water Rat much satisfaction but could involve him in more time and work than he first envisaged. He can, however, look forward to a noticeable upturn in his financial situation in 1996, but it would still be in his interests to watch his general level of expenditure. Although he prides himself on being careful in money matters, his level of outgoings could be greater than he thought. The Water Rat will do well in his work over the year and many Water Rats will take on new responsibilities or obtain a more interesting and challenging position. The Water Rat should pursue any opportunities that he sees, especially in the early months of the Rat year. He should also not be reticent about advancing his ideas or using any opportunities that he gets to widen his experience. This is a most constructive year for him and in addition to the progress he will make, the experience he gains will do much to help his future prospects. There will also be opportunities for Water Rats to travel quite extensively over the year and for any Water Rat who wishes to go abroad to improve on language skills or gain work experience, this could be an ideal year to do so. With his resourceful and positive nature, the year will hold many splendid opportunities for the Water Rat and it rests with him to take full advantage of the auspicious trends that prevail. The summer months are likely to be a particularly enjoyable time for him.

This will be a fulfilling year for the *Wood Rat* but during 1996 he does need to plan his activities with care. He should give some thought to what he wants to achieve during the year and then go after his objectives. If not, he could very easily drift through the year without achieving very much or making the most of his many talents. The Wood Rat will obtain much pleasure from his various interests over the year, especially any that enable him to use his creative or artistic skills. He could also find a new interest that he takes up most enjoyable – and, again, if it gives him an outlet for his creative talents, he is likely to find this will give him many hours of pleasure. By using any spare time he has constructively he will find the year will be one of the most enjoyable and stimulating that he has had for a long time. Those Wood Rats in education will make pleasing progress in their studies, although if they do have any matter concerning them – whether academic or personal – they would do well to talk to others rather than keep their worry to themselves. In many cases they could find their fears are groundless and that those around them are only too pleased to help and support them. The Wood Rat can also look forward to some memorable times with his family and friends and both domestically and socially he will be very much in demand. Financial matters will also go well and many Wood Rats will enjoy considerable good fortune in their financial dealings. However, the Wood Rat should exercise caution if he enters into any large financial transaction over the year and make sure that he is fully aware of any obligations he might be placed under. There will be several opportunities for the Wood Rat to travel over the year and the journeys and holidays that he takes are likely to go well. He should also take advantage of any chance he gets to meet up with friends or relations he has not seen for some years; such a meeting will give all concerned much pleasure. Generally, this will be a good year for the Wood Rat and if he plans his activities with care and uses his time constructively, he will find the year both satisfying and most enjoyable for him.

This is the Year of the Fire Rat and for the *Fire Rat* himself it will prove a memorable and significant year. It would be useful to him to start the year with some idea of what he wants to accomplish over the next 12 months – this can concern his work, his interests, his accommodation or some personal project – and once he has decided upon his priorities, he should set about achieving his aims. With a positive and purposeful attitude, the Fire Rat can accomplish much. His work, in particular, will give him much satisfaction and his past efforts and diligence will be well-rewarded and recognized by those with influence and authority. For those who wish, there will be opportunities for further career advancement, while others may choose to retire. In either case, the Fire Rat will be pleased with how events work out for him. The Fire Rat will also derive much satisfaction from his various hobbies over the year, particularly those that involve outdoor pursuits or allow him to meet others. If there has been an interest that has intrigued him in the past, this would be an ideal year to find out more. Many Fire Rats will obtain much enjoyment from new interests and skills that they take up and by using their time constructively, they can accomplish much. Those Fire Rats who change their accommodation in 1996 will be well pleased with how their move works out and could feel stimulated by being in a new environment and by the opportunity to make new friends and establish a new social life. Many will also occupy themselves carrying out projects around the home and the work they do will give them much pride and satisfaction. The Fire Rat can also look forward to having some most enjoyable times with his family and will take particular delight in the success and progress enjoyed by a younger relation. Generally, 1996 will be a good year for the Fire Rat.

However, he does need to sort out his priorities for the year and think about what he wishes to accomplish. With a positive and determined attitude, this can be a successful and fulfilling year for him.

This will be an important year for the *Earth Rat*. He can look forward to making substantial progress in his career and many Earth Rats will take on new responsibilities or move to a more challenging and rewarding position. Throughout the year, the Earth Rat, whether in work or seeking work, should remain alert for openings to pursue as well as chances to further his skills and ideas. Although he is a keen planner, he does not always like change, yet this year he should be bold and adventurous in his actions and take full advantage of the opportunities that become available. Several times during the year unexpected events will cause the Earth Rat to make important decisions and by being positive in his outlook he can make significant progress. The Earth Rat has many skills and talents and in 1996 he should make the most of them! Those close to the Earth Rat will be both encouraging and supportive over the year and if he has any uncertainties or is in a dilemma over any matter he should not hesitate to seek their advice. The Earth Rat's domestic life will be busy but will also bring him much pleasure and he will take particular delight in the achievements of someone close to him. However, over the year, he may have to assist a relation or close friend with an awkward problem. His considerate and under-standing manner will be much appreciated, as well as doing considerable good. The Earth Rat's social life will also be most enjoyable and any Earth Rat who may have been feeling lonely or dispirited would do well to go out more and try to build up a new social life. Anything positive he can do will be of great benefit to him. There will also be several opportunities for the Earth Rat to travel over the year and, while sometimes this could be at short notice, the journeys and holidays that he takes will prove both enjoyable and beneficial for him. Generally, 1996 will be a good year for the Earth Rat and it is a year which holds many excellent opportunities for him. Admittedly, some of these opportunities, especially in his work, could involve substantial changes, but these changes will bring new and stimulating challenges for the Earth Rat. With a bold and positive approach, this can be an important and significant year for him.

## FAMOUS RATS

Alan Alda, Dave Allen, Ursula Andress, Louis Armstrong, Charles Aznavour, Lauren Bacall, Shirley Bassey, Jeremy Beadle, Irving Berlin, Silvio Berlusconi, Virginia Bottomley, Kenneth Branagh, Marlon Brando, Charlotte Brontë, Chris de Burgh, George Bush, Lord Callaghan, Jimmy Carter, Pablo Casals, Dick Cavett, Raymond Chandler, Maurice Chevalier, Linford Christie, Barbara Dickson, Benjamin Disraeli, Noël Edmonds, T. S. Eliot, Ben Elton, Albert Finney, Clark Gable, Al Gore, Thomas Hardy, Vaclav Havel, Charlton Heston, Damon Hill, Dennis Hopper, Roy Hudd, Engelbert Humperdinck, Jeremy Irons, Glenda Jackson, Jean-Michel Jarre, Gene Kelly, F. W. de Klerk, Kris Kristofferson, Lawrence of Arabia, Gary Lineker, Andrew Lloyd Webber, Lulu, Henri Mancini,

Claude Monet, Earl Mountbatten, Robert Mugabe, Richard Nixon, Robert Palmer, Sean Penn, Enoch Powell, the Queen Mother, Vanessa Redgrave, Burt Reynolds, Jonathan Ross, Rossini, Emma Samms, William Shakespeare, Wayne Sleep, Yves St Laurent, Tommy Steele, Donna Summer, James Taylor, Leo Tolstoy, Spencer Tracey, the Prince of Wales, George Washington, Dennis Waterman, Dennis Weaver, Roger Whittaker, Kim Wilde, Bill Wyman, the Duke of York, Emile Zola.

| | |
|---|---|
| 19 FEBRUARY 1901 ～ 7 FEBRUARY 1902 | *Metal Ox* |
| 6 FEBRUARY 1913 ～ 24 JANUARY 1914 | *Water Ox* |
| 25 JANUARY 1925 ～ 12 FEBRUARY 1926 | *Wood Ox* |
| 11 FEBRUARY 1937 ～ 30 JANUARY 1938 | *Fire Ox* |
| 29 JANUARY 1949 ～ 16 FEBRUARY 1950 | *Earth Ox* |
| 15 FEBRUARY 1961 ～ 4 FEBRUARY 1962 | *Metal Ox* |
| 3 FEBRUARY 1973 ～ 22 JANUARY 1974 | *Water Ox* |
| 20 FEBRUARY 1985 ～ 8 FEBRUARY 1986 | *Wood Ox* |

# THE
# OX

# THE PERSONALITY OF THE OX

To know oneself, one should assert oneself.

*– Albert Camus: an Ox*

The Ox is born under the signs of equilibrium and tenacity. He is a hard and conscientious worker and sets about everything he does in a resolute, methodical and determined manner. He has considerable leadership qualities and is often admired for his tough and uncompromising nature. He knows what he wants to achieve in life and, as far as possible, will not be deflected from his ultimate objective.

The Ox takes his responsibilities and duties very seriously. He is decisive and quick to take advantage of any opportunity that comes his way. He is also sincere and places a great deal of trust in his friends and colleagues. He is, nevertheless, something of a loner. He is a quiet and private individual and often keeps his thoughts to himself. He also cherishes his independence and prefers to set about things in his own way rather than be bound by the dictates of others or be influenced by outside pressures.

The Ox tends to have a calm and tranquil nature, but if something angers him or he feels that someone has let him down, he can have a fearsome temper. He can also be stubborn and obstinate and this can lead him into conflict with others. Usually the Ox will succeed in getting his own way, but should things go against him, he is a poor loser and will take any defeat or set-back extremely badly.

The Ox is often a deep thinker and rather studious. He is not particularly renowned for his sense of humour and

24

does not take kindly to new gimmicks or anything too innovative. The Ox is too solid and traditional for that and he prefers to stick to the more conventional norm.

His home is very important to him and in some respects he treats it as a private sanctuary. His family tends to be closely knit and the Ox will make sure that each member does their fair share around the house. The Ox tends to be a hoarder, but he is always well-organized and neat. He also places great importance on punctuality and there is nothing that infuriates him more than to be kept waiting – particularly if it is due to someone's inefficiency. The Ox can be a hard taskmaster!

Once settled in a job or house the Ox will quite happily remain there for many years. He does not like change and he is also not particularly keen on travel. He does, however, enjoy gardening and other outdoor pursuits and he will often spend much of his spare time out of doors. The Ox is usually an excellent gardener and whenever possible he will always make sure he has a large area of ground to maintain. The Ox usually prefers to live in the country rather than the town.

Due to his dedicated and dependable nature, he will usually do well in his chosen career, providing he is given enough freedom to act on his own initiative. He invariably does well in politics, agriculture and in careers which need specialized training. The Ox is also very gifted in the arts and many Oxen have enjoyed considerable success as musicians or composers.

The Ox is not as outgoing as some and it often takes him a long time to establish friendships and feel relaxed in another person's company. His courtships are likely to be long, but once he is settled he will remain devoted and loyal to his partner. The Ox is particularly well-suited to those born under the signs of the Rat, Rabbit, Snake and Rooster. He can also establish a good relationship with the Monkey, Dog, Pig and another Ox, but he will find that he has little in common with the whimsical and sensitive Goat. He will also find it difficult to get on with the Horse, Dragon and Tiger – the Ox prefers a quiet and peaceful existence and those born under these three signs tend to be a little too lively and impulsive for his liking.

The female Ox has a kind and caring nature, and her home and family are very much her pride and joy. She always tries to do her best for her partner and can be a most conscientious and loving parent. She is an excellent organizer and also a very determined person who will often succeed in getting what she wants in life. She usually has a deep interest in the arts and is often a talented artist or musician.

The Ox is a very down-to-earth character. He is sincere, loyal and unpretentious. He can, however, be rather reserved and to some he may appear distant and aloof. He has a quiet nature, but underneath he is very strong-willed and ambitious. He has the courage of his convictions and is often prepared to stand up for what he believes is right, regardless of the consequences. He inspires confidence and trust and throughout his life he will rarely be short of people who are ready to support him or who admire his strong and resolute manner.

# THE FIVE DIFFERENT TYPES OF OX

In addition to the 12 signs of the Chinese zodiac, there are five elements and these have a strengthening or moderating influence on the sign. The effects of the five elements on the Ox are described below, together with the years in which the elements were exercising their influence. Therefore all Oxen born in 1901 and 1961 are Metal Oxen, those born in 1913 and 1973 are Water Oxen, and so on.

## Metal Ox: 1901, 1961
This Ox is confident and very strong-willed. He can be blunt and forthright in his views and is not afraid of speaking his mind. He sets about his objectives with a dogged determination, but he can become so wrapped up in his various activities that he can be oblivious to the thoughts and feelings of those around him, and this can sometimes be to his detriment. He is honest and dependable and will never promise more than he can deliver. He has a good appreciation of the arts and usually has a small circle of very good and loyal friends.

## Water Ox: 1913, 1973
This Ox has a sharp and penetrating mind. He is a good organizer and sets about his work in a methodical manner. He is not as narrow-minded as some of the other types of Oxen and is more willing to involve others in his plans and aspirations. He usually has very high moral standards and is often attracted to careers in public service. He is a good

judge of character and has such a friendly and persuasive manner that he usually experiences little difficulty in securing his objectives. He is popular and has an excellent way with children.

## Wood Ox: 1925, 1985

The Wood Ox conducts himself with an air of dignity and authority and will often take a leading role in any enterprise in which he gets involved. He is very self-confident and is direct in his dealings with others. He does, however, have a quick temper and has no hesitation in speaking his mind. He has tremendous drive and will-power and has an extremely good memory. The Wood Ox is particularly loyal and devoted to the members of his family and has a most caring nature.

## Fire Ox: 1937

The Fire Ox has a powerful and assertive personality and is a hard and conscientious worker. He holds strong views and has very little patience when things do not go his own way. He can also get carried away in the excitement of the moment and does not always take into account the views of those around him. He nevertheless has many leadership qualities and will often reach positions of power, eminence and wealth. He usually has a small group of loyal and close friends and is very devoted to his family.

## Earth Ox: 1949

This Ox sets about everything he does in a sensible and level-headed manner. He is ambitious, but he is also realistic in his aims and is often prepared to work long hours in order to secure his objectives. He is shrewd in financial and business matters and is a very good judge of character. He has a quiet nature and is greatly admired for his sincerity and integrity. He is also very loyal to his family and friends and his views and opinions are often sought by others.

# PROSPECTS FOR THE OX IN 1996

The Chinese New Year starts on 19 February 1996. Until then, the old year, the Year of the Pig, is still making its presence felt.

The Year of the Pig (31 January 1995 to 18 February 1996) will have been an interesting and active year for the Ox, with the latter part of the year being a most constructive time for him. In the closing stages of the Pig year the Ox can accomplish much, both in his work and his home life, but in both cases he does need to handle his relations with others with care. In all his activities he needs to remain mindful of the views and feelings of those around him and not adopt too independent an attitude. Sometimes he can be just a little too independent in his actions and this could hamper his progress. Also, in the interests of domestic harmony, the Ox should avoid getting so preoccupied with his own concerns that he does not spend as much time with his family and friends as he should. If he is not careful, this could lead to some tensions. In the months from November 1995 to January 1996 the Ox needs to be more forthcoming, to be willing to join in with others and to listen carefully to those around him. If he can bear this in mind, the end of the Pig year will be a most pleasant time for him.

Similarly, if the Ox has experienced any difficulties or strains in his relations with someone, either a family member or work colleague, he would do well to use the closing months of the year to sort out any remaining differences. He will find that by tackling any existing problem in a conciliatory and understanding matter he will do much to sort it out. In the last few months of the Pig year the Ox's relations with others can go well, but care and forethought are needed.

The Ox will also make some pleasing progress in his work towards the end of the year and financial matters too are well aspected. In particular, he should remain alert for bargains in the shops, especially in late December and in January. He could make some excellent purchases both for his home and himself at this time. Generally, the Ox will have accomplished much in the Pig year and gained a lot of useful experience. In the new Chinese year he will be able to put his gains to good use.

The Year of the Rat starts on 19 February and is going to be a favourable year for the Ox. He can look forward to making progress in many of his activities as well as enjoying several strokes of good fortune.

During the year the Ox should continue to set about his activities in his usual purposeful way. In his work he will greatly impress others and many Oxen will be promoted or given new and more challenging responsibilities. The Ox has many talents and abilities and in the Rat year he should make the most of them. He should advance any ideas that he has and also take advantage of any new opportunities and situations that arise. Sometimes the Ox can be rather resistant to change and lose out on opportunities because of his overly cautious attitude. In 1996 he should try not to let his reticence mar his progress. By being both flexible and adaptable in his outlook he can make considerable progress, particularly in the autumn months.

Any Ox who is dissatisfied with his present position or is seeking work should remain alert for opportunities to pursue. Many Oxen will find their persistence and determination will be rewarded and if they are able to add to their skills at this time, they will find that this will do much to enhance their prospects.

The Rat year is also an excellent year for the Ox to launch new projects and further his ideas and if there is something that he has been thinking about for some time, now would be an ideal time to act. He can accomplish much in 1996, but it does rest with him to take the initiative. For those Oxen who are prepared to be bold, the rewards of the year can be considerable.

The Ox will also be helped by the supportive and encouraging attitudes of those around him, and he would do well to fully involve them in his plans and schemes. In 1996 he can gain much from the input and suggestions of others.

The Ox will also do well in financial matters and many

Oxen will receive a financial gift or unexpected bonus during the course of the year. The Ox could also enjoy some success with an investment that he makes or find that a savings scheme he starts will build into a worthwhile asset in years to come. The Ox is usually prudent and careful in financial matters and his shrewd judgement is likely to pay off handsomely in 1996.

Another area which is well aspected is travel and the Ox will thoroughly enjoy the journeys, holidays and breaks that he takes over the year. All Oxen should try to ensure that they go away at least once in 1996; they will feel much better for the rest and change of scene that a holiday gives them.

The Ox's domestic and social life will also bring him much pleasure and he can look forward to having some memorable times with his family and friends. Those close to him will do much to help and support him but, as always, the Ox does need to remain mindful of their views and involve them in his activities. He will, however, take much satisfaction in the accomplishments of a close relation over the year and many Oxen will also take delight in meeting up with relations or friends they have not seen for some considerable time.

The Ox will also lead a most fulfilling social life in 1996 and some social events that he attends – sometimes with misgivings – will prove unexpectedly pleasurable. They could enable him to meet and discuss his views and ideas with others. Something of considerable significance could develop from a chance meeting at a social occasion.

For the unattached Ox, or any Ox seeking friends, this can be a good year. Again, often quite unexpectedly, a chance meeting could lead to an important friendship. Romance and matters of the heart are well aspected, especially in the months from April to late June.

The Ox would also do well to make sure that he sets a regular time aside for his hobbies and interests. Although there may be times when he feels there are more pressing things to do, he should still not neglect his recreational interests. They do provide him with an important opportunity to unwind and will also bring him much satisfaction. If the Ox does not have an interest he can turn his attention to at an odd moment, he would do well to take one up. He could find a new activity both absorbing and therapeutic for him.

Generally, this will be a positive year for the Ox and he can accomplish much in almost all areas of his life. Financial matters are well aspected and there will be some excellent opportunities for him to pursue in his work, particularly arising out of changes that take place around him. However, in 1996 the Ox should resolve to make the most of his abilities and be willing to adapt to new situations. He should also remain mindful of the advice and views of others and, while he does like to retain a certain independence in his actions, he would be greatly assisted if he were more prepared to involve others in his ideas and plans. The aspects are most favourable for the Ox and it rests with him to take advantage of the considerable opportunities that the Rat year will bring.

As far as the different types of Ox are concerned, 1996 will be a significant year for the *Metal Ox*. The Metal Ox has many admirable talents and in 1996 he should resolve to make the most of them. He should promote his ideas and also remain alert for any new opportunities that arise. Many Metal Oxen will take on additional responsibilities in their work or be successful in obtaining a new and more rewarding position. Work matters are most favourably aspected throughout the year, particularly in the second half of 1996. The Metal Ox will also enjoy a substantial improvement in his financial situation, although he could be involved in some expense connected with his home and may need to budget accordingly. The Metal Ox's family will bring him much joy over the year and he can look forward to some splendid times with those around him. A family holiday he takes is likely to be one of the most pleasurable he has had for some time. His social life too will bring him much pleasure and a recent friendship he has built up is likely to prove especially important. In particular, some advice he is given by a close friend could prove most helpful to him and he would do well to listen carefully to what he is told. There will be much wisdom in their words. With the demands of his work and his generally busy home life, the Metal Ox may feel that he cannot spend as much time on his hobbies and interests as he would like. However, he does need to ensure that he sets a regular time aside for recreational interests and gives himself the opportunity to rest and unwind. If not, he could find himself becoming tired, tense and irritable, and not making the most of himself or his abilities. Also, if he does not take much exercise during the day, he could find that some extra physical activity could do much to improve his sense of well-being. Generally, 1996 will be a most positive year for the Metal Ox and he can accomplish much. He has many talents and fine qualities and these will be much appreciated during the year. This will be a year of progress as well as one of many happy and enjoyable times. The second half of 1996 in particular will be an active and progressive period for him.

This will be both a busy and enjoyable year for the *Water Ox*. His family and domestic life will be a great source of joy to him and he can look forward to some splendid and memorable times with those around him. Many Water Oxen will get engaged, married or see an addition to their family over the year. The months from May to August are particularly auspicious for personal matters. Throughout the year, however, the Water Ox does need to remain mindful of the views of those around him – particularly those of older relatives – and he should listen carefully to any advice that they give him. Although he may not agree with all he is told, he should remember that they do speak with experience and have his best interests at heart. Accommodation matters will also take up much of the Water Ox's time over the year. Some Water Oxen will carry out extensive alterations and improvements to their home while others will move. In either case the whole process will take longer and prove more costly than the Water Ox may have anticipated, but he will be well pleased with the result. With his practical nature and creative skills, he will find any DIY projects that he carries out around his house most satisfying. The Water Ox will also make substantial progress in his work. He should not hesitate to advance any ideas that he has or pursue any opportunities and vacancies that interest him. Although not all his efforts may meet with total success, throughout the year he will be adding to his experience and this will do much to enhance his prospects in later years. Many Water Oxen will take on new responsibilities as the year progresses. The Water Ox will also be given much practical help and support by his colleagues and those who recognize his potential. This too will assist his progress. He will also enjoy some good fortune in financial matters, although if he does get involved in any large financial transaction, he does need to make sure he is aware of all the obligations he might be placed under. There will be several opportunities for him to travel over the year and for any Water Ox who would like to improve upon his language skills or widen his experience by working abroad, this would be an ideal year to do so. Generally, 1996 will be a favourable year for the Water Ox and he will not only obtain much useful experience in his work but personally the year will contain some most memorable times for him. The Rat year will be a year the Water Ox will very much enjoy.

This will be a satisfying and generally enjoyable year for the *Wood Ox*. His domestic and social life will give him much pleasure and he will have good reason to be proud of the achievements of someone very close to him. The Wood Ox can also look forward to attending several memorable social functions over the year and these will give him the opportunity to add to his circle of friends and acquaintances. The Wood Ox's hobbies and interests will also give him much satisfaction and many Wood Oxen could find that they are able to put a skill or talent to some profitable use. This year will contain several pleasant surprises for the Wood Ox and at all times he should advance his ideas and pursue any opportunities that he spots. He will find that positive action, combined with constructive use of his time, will lead to worthwhile results. The Wood Ox will also enjoy any holidays that he takes, although he would do well to plan his trips away with care. He should make sure he is conversant with all the connections involved and that he goes away adequately prepared. If not, some over-sight could take the edge off his time away. The Wood Ox will be fortunate in financial matters over the year and by remaining alert he could purchase some items at most advantageous prices. The Wood Ox has a shrewd eye when it comes to spotting bargains! While much of the year will go in his favour, there may be some matters – particularly of a bureaucratic nature – that could give him cause for concern. If he does have any worries, he should not hesi-tate to seek the advice of others rather than keeping the worry to himself. In some instances he could find he is worrying unnecessarily. Also, those Wood Oxen involved in education could experience several changes over the year – this could involve changing schools or starting new subjects – and again if the Wood Ox is troubled by any of the changes that take place he would do well to speak of his concern. He will find those around him most understanding and supportive. Generally, 1996 will be a pleasing year for the Wood Ox and by using his time constructively he will be delighted with what he is able to accomplish. The summer months will be a particularly active and fulfilling time for him.

This will be an eventful year for the *Fire Ox* and over the year several significant changes will take place. These changes could particularly concern his work and daily activities. Over the year the Fire Ox will have several important decisions to take – this could involve taking on newer and greater responsibilities, transferring to a different type of work or retiring. In all cases the Fire Ox should not allow himself to be rushed into taking any irrevocable decision or be forced into taking any action against his better judgement. Time is on his side and he should think over the options available and talk to his family and colleagues. He will be grateful for their support and advice and will be satisfied with the decision that he finally does take. However, in 1996 the Fire Ox must be prepared to adapt to new situations as they occur as well as remain mindful of the views of those around him. Sometimes his intransigence can undermine his progress and he should not allow this to happen in this important and generally auspicious year for him. The Fire Ox will enjoy good fortune in financial matters and many Fire Oxen will receive an additional sum of money over the year, either from work which they have carried out in the past or as the fruition of an investment. If the Fire Ox is able to re-invest some of this money, he could find it will prove particularly useful to him in future years. The Fire Ox will take much delight in his home life over the year and will be much in demand with both his family and friends. Travel is also well aspected and a holiday that he takes during the summer will prove most enjoyable, particularly if it is to an area he has not visited before. The Fire Ox would also do well to set some time aside over the year to take up an additional interest or learn a new skill. He will find that this will be a stimulating challenge for him as well as giving him many hours of pleasure. In addition to this, projects that he carries out in his home and garden are likely to bring both him and those around him much satisfaction. Generally, this will be an important and favourable year for the Fire Ox and while some decisions that he has to take, particularly concerning his future, will cause him some anguish, the events of the year will move in his favour. If he can use his free time constructively, the Fire Ox will feel well satisfied with what he is able to accomplish.

This will be a positive year for the *Earth Ox*. Over the last few years he will have impressed many with his skills and diligence as well as gaining much useful experience; in 1996 he will be able to reap his rewards. In his work the Earth Ox can make significant progress and he should promote his skills, ideas and talents as much as he can. Those around him will prove most supportive and by acting positively and pursuing any opportunities that he sees, the Earth Ox can enjoy considerable success. Many Earth Oxen will move to a more interesting and challenging position over the year or be given more rewarding responsibilities. For those Earth Oxen seeking work or wanting a change in their work, there will be several excellent opportunities to pursue and by following up any openings that they see they will find their persistence rewarded. The months of March, September, October and November could prove particularly significant for career matters. The Earth Ox will also enjoy a substantial upturn in his financial situation over the year, although he would do well to save some of the money he is able to accumulate. If he is able to invest in some long-term saving scheme he could find this will build into a useful asset in years to come. The Earth Ox will, however, spend both time and money on projects around his home and he will be well pleased with the work he is able to carry out. He can also look forward to some splendid times with his family and friends and many will have good cause for a celebration. This could be an engagement or wedding or the birth of a grandchild. A younger relation in particular will be a great source of pride to him. The Earth Ox will also obtain much satisfaction from his hobbies and interests over the year and if he has any of a creative nature he would do well to further his skills and promote his work. He will find his efforts well received and they could lead to some unexpected opportunities. Indeed, throughout the year the Earth Ox should not be reticent about promoting himself or his talents. This is a very positive year for him and by being bold, assertive and enterprising, he will not only accomplish much but also benefit from some of the surprises and unexpected opportunities that the year holds for him.

# FAMOUS OXEN

Hans Christian Andersen, Johann Sebastian Bach, Warren Beatty, Menachem Begin, Tony Benn, Jon Bon Jovi, Napoleon Bonaparte, Rory Bremner, Jeff Bridges, Benjamin Britten, Frank Bruno, Richard Burton, Barbara Bush, Johnny Carson, Barbara Cartland, Judith Chalmers, Charlie Chaplin, Warren Christopher, George Cole, Natalie Cole, Bill Cosby, Tom Courtenay, Tony Curtis, Sammy Davis Jr, Jacques Delors, Donald Dewar, Walt Disney, Patrick Duffy, Harry Enfield, Jane Fonda, Michael Foot, Gerald Ford,

Edward Fox, Michael J. Fox, Peter Gabriel, Richard Gere, Whoopi Goldberg, George Frederick Handel, Robert Hardy, King Harold V of Norway, Nigel Havers, Mariel Hemingway, Adolf Hitler, Dustin Hoffman, Anthony Hopkins, Saddam Hussein, Billy Joel, Don Johnson, Jack Jones, King Juan Carlos of Spain, Penny Junor, B. B. King, Mark Knopfler, Burt Lancaster, Jessica Lange, Angela Lansbury, Jack Lemmon, Nicholas Lyndhurst, David Mellor, Warren Mitchell, Mary Tyler Moore, Alison Moyet, Eddie Murphy, Jawaharlal Nehru, Paul Newman, Jack Nicholson, Leslie Nielsen, Billy Ocean, Oscar Peterson, Colin Powell, Robert Redford, Peter Paul Rubens, Willie Rushton, Meg Ryan, Arthur Scargill, Monica Seles, Peter Sellers, Jean Sibelius, Jimmy Somerville, Sissy Spacek, Bruce Springsteen, Rod Steiger, Meryl Streep, Elaine Stritch, Loretta Swit, Lady Thatcher, Mel Torme, Twiggy, Dick Van Dyke, the Princess of Wales, Zoë Wanamaker, the Duke of Wellington, Alan Whicker, June Whitfield, Barbara Windsor, Ernie Wise, W. B. Yeats.

| | | |
|---|---|---|
| 8 FEBRUARY 1902 ∽ 28 JANUARY 1903 | | *Water Tiger* |
| 25 JANUARY 1914 ∽ 13 FEBRUARY 1915 | | *Wood Tiger* |
| 13 FEBRUARY 1926 ∽ 1 FEBRUARY 1927 | | *Fire Tiger* |
| 31 JANUARY 1938 ∽ 18 FEBRUARY 1939 | | *Earth Tiger* |
| 17 FEBRUARY 1950 ∽ 5 FEBRUARY 1951 | | *Metal Tiger* |
| 5 FEBRUARY 1962 ∽ 24 JANUARY 1963 | | *Water Tiger* |
| 23 JANUARY 1974 ∽ 10 FEBRUARY 1975 | | *Wood Tiger* |
| 9 FEBRUARY 1986 ∽ 28 JANUARY 1987 | | *Fire Tiger* |

# THE
# TIGER

# THE PERSONALITY OF THE TIGER

Not knowing when the dawn will come, I open every door.

*– Emily Dickinson: a Tiger*

The Tiger is born under the sign of courage. He is a charismatic figure and usually holds very firm views and beliefs. He is strong-willed and determined, and sets about most of the things he does with a tremendous energy and enthusiasm. He is very alert and quick-witted and his mind is forever active. He is a highly original thinker and is nearly always brimming with new ideas or full of enthusiasm for some new project or scheme.

The Tiger adores challenges and he loves to get involved in anything which he thinks has an exciting future or which catches his imagination. He is prepared to take risks and does not like to be bound either by convention or the dictates of others. The Tiger likes to be free to act as he chooses and at least once during his life he will throw caution to the wind and go off and do the things he wants to do.

The Tiger does, however, have a somewhat restless nature. Even though he is often prepared to throw himself wholeheartedly into a project, his initial enthusiasm can soon wane if he sees something more appealing. He can also be rather impulsive and there will be occasions in his life when he acts in a manner which he later regrets. If the Tiger were to think things out or to persevere in his various activities, he would almost certainly enjoy a greater degree of success.

Fortunately, the Tiger is lucky in most of his enterprises, but should things not work out as he had hoped, he is liable to suffer from severe bouts of depression and it will often take him a long time to recover. The Tiger's life often consists of a series of ups and downs.

The Tiger is, however, very adaptable. He has an adventurous spirit and rarely stays in the same place for long. In the early stages of his life he is likely to try his hand at several different jobs and he will also change his residence fairly frequently.

The Tiger is very honest and open in his dealings with others. He hates any sort of hypocrisy or falsehood. He is also well known for being blunt and forthright and has no hesitation in speaking his mind. He can also be most rebellious at times, particularly against any form of petty authority, and while this can lead the Tiger into conflict with others, he is never one to shrink from an argument or avoid standing up for what he believes is right.

The Tiger is a natural leader and can invariably rise to the top of his chosen profession. He does not, however, care for anything too bureaucratic or detailed and he also does not like to obey orders. He can be stubborn and obstinate, and throughout his life he likes to retain a certain amount of independence in his actions and be responsible to no one but himself. He likes to consider that all his achievements are due to his own efforts and unless he cannot avoid it, he will rarely ask for support from others.

Ironically, despite his self-confidence and leadership qualities, the Tiger can be indecisive and will often delay making a major decision until the very last moment. He can also be sensitive to criticism.

Although the Tiger is capable of earning large sums of money, he is rather a spendthrift and does not always put his money to its best use. He can also be most generous and will often shower lavish gifts on friends and relations.

The Tiger cares very much for his reputation and the image that he tries to project. He carries himself with an air of dignity and authority and enjoys being the centre of attention. He is very adept at attracting publicity, both for himself and for the causes he supports.

The Tiger often marries young and he will find himself best suited to those born under the signs of the Pig, Dog, Horse and Goat. He can also get on well with the Rat, Rabbit and Rooster, but will find the Ox and Snake a bit too quiet and too serious for his liking, and he will also be highly irritated by the Monkey's rather mischievous and inquisitive ways. The Tiger will also find it difficult to get on with another Tiger or a Dragon – both partners will want to dominate the relationship and could find it difficult to compromise on even the smallest of matters.

The Tigress is lively, witty and a marvellous hostess at parties. She is usually most attractive and takes great care over her appearance. She can also be a very doting mother and while she believes in letting her children have their freedom, she makes an excellent teacher and will ensure that her children are brought up well and want for nothing. Like her male counterpart, she has numerous interests and likes to have sufficient independence and freedom to go off and do the things that she wants to do. She also has a most caring and generous nature.

The Tiger has many commendable qualities. He is honest, courageous and often a source of inspiration for others. Providing he can curb the wilder excesses of his restless nature, he is almost certain to lead a most fulfilling and satisfying life.

# THE FIVE DIFFERENT TYPES OF TIGER

In addition to the 12 signs of the Chinese zodiac, there are five elements and these have a strengthening or moderating influence on the sign. The effects of the five elements on the Tiger are described below, together with the years in which the elements were exercising their influence. Therefore all Tigers born in 1950 are Metal Tigers, those born in 1902 and 1962 are Water Tigers, and so on.

## Metal Tiger: 1950

The Metal Tiger has an assertive and outgoing personality. He is very ambitious and, while his aims may change from time to time, he will work relentlessly until he has obtained what he wants. He can, however, be impatient for results and also get highly strung if things do not work out as he would like. He is distinctive in his appearance and is admired and respected by many.

## Water Tiger: 1902, 1962

This Tiger has a wide variety of interests and is always eager to experiment with new ideas or go off and explore distant lands. He is versatile, shrewd and has a kindly nature. The Water Tiger tends to remain calm in a crisis, although he can be annoyingly indecisive at times. He communicates well with others and through his many capabilities and persuasive nature he usually achieves what he wants in life. He is also highly imaginative and is often a gifted orator or writer.

## Wood Tiger: 1914, 1974

The Wood Tiger has a very friendly and pleasant personality. He is less independent than some of the other types of Tiger and is more prepared to work with others to secure a desired objective. However, he does have a tendency to jump from one thing to another and can get easily distracted. He is usually very popular, has a large circle of friends and invariably leads a busy and enjoyable social life. He also has a good sense of humour.

## Fire Tiger: 1926, 1986

The Fire Tiger sets about everything he does with great verve and enthusiasm. He loves action and is always ready to throw himself wholeheartedly into anything which catches his imagination. He has many leadership qualities and is capable of communicating his ideas and enthusiasm to others. He is very much an optimist and can be most generous. He has a likeable nature and can be a witty and persuasive speaker.

*Earth Tiger: 1938*
This Tiger is responsible and level-headed. He studies
everything objectively and tries to be scrupulously fair in
all his dealings. Unlike other Tigers, he is prepared to
specialize in certain areas rather than get distracted by
other matters, but he can become so involved with what he
is doing that he does not always take into account the
views and opinions of those around him. He has good business sense and is usually very successful in later life. He
has a large circle of friends and pays great attention to both
his appearance and his reputation.

# PROSPECTS FOR THE TIGER
# IN 1996

The Chinese New Year starts on 19 February 1996. Until
then, the old year, the Year of the Pig, is still making its
presence felt.

The Year of the Pig (31 January 1995 to 18 February
1996) will have been a generally favourable year for the
Tiger. In what remains of the Pig year the Tiger should
make the most of his many talents. He should advance his
ideas and actively pursue any openings that are available to
him, especially in his work. The latter part of the Pig year
is a positive time for him and he should make the most of
the prevailing trends. The bold and enterprising Tiger's
accomplishments can be considerable in the last few
months of the year.

The Tiger does, however, need to exercise care in financial matters and keep a close watch on his level of expenditure. To stretch his resources too far could cause problems later. Also, he should be wary of any speculative enterprises that he hears about. The Pig year is not a year when the Tiger can take financial risks. Care is also needed in making travel arrangements and the Tiger should make sure he has all the connections sorted out before he leaves on any lengthy journey.

The Tiger can, however, look forward to some splendid times with his loved ones and he will thoroughly enjoy the social events that he attends towards the end of the year. He would, however, do well to remain mindful of the views of those around him and pay heed to any advice he is given. Something that the Tiger is told or learns about in December 1995 or January 1996 could prove most significant to him over the next year.

Generally, the last few months of the Pig year will be both enjoyable and constructive for the Tiger and he should do all he can to pursue his ideas and promote his talents, as well as enjoy the happy times he will have with his family and friends.

The Year of the Rat starts on 19 February and is going to be a variable year for the Tiger. He could find his progress slow and not all his plans will work out in the manner he would like. However, while the Rat year may not be the best of years for the Tiger, he can still turn this into a constructive and significant time. The Tiger is blessed with many fine qualities: he is enterprising, has a wide range of talents and is capable of much original thought. These talents, together with his resourcefulness, will help him greatly over the Rat year.

In 1996 the Tiger needs to plan his activities carefully and decide upon his priorities and objectives. This is not a year when he can spread his energies too widely. He will find his best results will come from planning and concentrating his efforts on areas that he is familiar with. In his work the Tiger will need to proceed carefully and at all times bear in mind the views of others. Although the Tiger does like to retain a certain independence in his actions, this is not a year in which he can act alone or without the backing of others. If he does, he could find himself isolated and lacking the support he needs. Similarly, if he has any problems in his work, he would do well to seek the advice of others rather than shoulder the difficulty all by himself. In all his activities the Tiger does need to work closely with others and curb his independent tendencies. He should also try not to be too impatient for results – progress is possible and will come, but it will take time and persistence.

While the Tiger will need to act cautiously over the year, he should still put forward any ideas that he has, and if he sees any opportunities for advancement, he should follow these up. Similarly, those Tigers seeking work or wanting to move to another position should remain alert for any openings to pursue, particularly in the first half of the year. Also, all Tigers would do well to widen their experience in some way and take advantage of any training courses that they might be eligible for. Anything positive that the Tiger can do to enhance his future prospects will be in his interest.

The Tiger will again need to exercise caution in financial matters over the year. He would do well to keep a watchful eye over his level of expenditure and if he is experiencing any financial problems, he should carry out a review of all his outgoings and make any modifications he feels are necessary. Sometimes the Tiger can be indulgent and a spendthrift and in 1996 he will need to take care with his spending. If he does get involved in a major financial transaction, he needs to make sure he understands all the terms and implications, and if he has any doubts, he should seek professional advice. Provided he is careful all will be well, but generally this is not a year in which he can take risks with his money.

The Tiger's domestic and social life will, however, bring him considerable pleasure. His family will give him much support and encouragement and again he would do well to discuss his views, feelings and ideas with them. His loved ones want to help and support him, but for them to be able to do this, the Tiger does need to make every effort to involve them in his activities. His family life will, though, give him much satisfaction and he will take much delight in the achievements of those close to him, especially a younger relation. Any additional support he feels able to give will be truly appreciated.

The Tiger's social life will also go well and he will attend several memorable parties and functions over the year. He will have the opportunity to extend his circle of friends and acquaintances and some of those he meets will prove of considerable help to him over the next few years. The unattached Tiger will lead a lively social life over the year and there will be many opportunities for meeting others and for romance. However, matters of the heart do need careful handling and the Tiger would do well to let any new romance proceed gradually rather than build up high expectations after just a short meeting.

The Tiger will enjoy the travelling that he undertakes over the year and any holidays or breaks are likely to go well, particularly if they are to places he has not visited before and appeal to his adventurous nature. Travel is well aspected in 1996, especially over the summer months.

The Tiger will also obtain much satisfaction from his various hobbies and interests, and he would do well to consider getting in contact with others who share them, perhaps by joining a local club or society. This will not only lead to new friendships but could also extend his interests quite considerably. Creative and outdoor pursuits in particular are likely to give the Tiger much pleasure over the year.

Generally, many Tigers tend to keep themselves fit with their active lifestyle but any who do not get much daily exercise should make sure they do not neglect their own well-being. They could find some additional exercise such as walking, cycling or swimming especially beneficial and those who are reliant on fast and convenience food could find switching to a more balanced diet to their advantage.

Although 1996 will be a variable year for the Tiger, it will still hold some pleasurable times for him. His family and social life will give him much pleasure and so too will his interests and the travelling that he undertakes. However, he does need to be cautious when dealing with his work and with financial matters. This is not a year for taking risks or pushing his luck too far. The Tiger needs to concentrate on specific areas and proceed carefully and cautiously. Also, if he is able to add to his skills and experience over the year, he will find that this will stand him in good stead for the future.

As far as the different types of Tiger are concerned, 1996 will be a challenging year for the *Metal Tiger*. Over the year he could find progress difficult; some of his plans and ideas may have to be altered or deferred. Some of the year will prove intensely frustrating for the Metal Tiger, particularly as he tends to be ambitious and so desirous to get things done. However, despite any setbacks, delays and problems that he may face, this can still be a valuable year for him. In 1996 he will be able to take stock of his current situation and think carefully about his future aims and aspirations. If he meets with obstacles, this again could help him to reflect on what he is trying to achieve and to re-think and often improve upon his ideas. Throughout the year he would do well to discuss his plans with others and listen carefully to all he is told. He will be given much useful advice in 1996 and a long-standing friend could prove particularly helpful to him. As with all Tigers, the Metal Tiger will need to proceed carefully and cautiously in his work. He should avoid taking unnecessary risks or acting without the support of others. He can make progress over the year, as well as usefully extend his experience, but this is not a year when he can take unnecessary chances. Similarly, the Metal Tiger will also need to keep a close watch over his level of expenditure. Without care he could find this is greater than he thought and if he plans to make an expensive purchase he should make sure he budgets accordingly. If not, he could find he is biting deep into his savings and they could be hard to replenish. The Metal Tiger will, however, obtain much pleasure from his family and social life and both will keep him busy and well-occupied. He will be delighted with the success enjoyed by a younger relation and he can also look forward to some pleasurable family occasions. In particular a holiday that he takes during the summer will be one of the best he has had for a long time. The Metal Tiger will lead a pleasant social life and his interests and hobbies too will be an important source of relaxation for him, particularly if they take him out-of-doors. Although the Metal Tiger's level of progress may not be as great as he would like over the year, 1996 will still contain some happy and memorable times for him.

This will be an interesting year for the *Water Tiger*. He will need to set about his activities with care and some of his ideas may not come to fruition, but he will still be able to make a modest amount of progress. In all his activities he should give of his best, remain mindful of the views of others and also be prepared to adapt to changing situations. In 1996 he will gain much valuable experience as well as learn much about himself and his abilities. Some of the events that happen will also do much to strengthen his character and resolve and he will emerge from the year a wiser, more assertive and stronger person. The year could also help him to review his present position and think hard about his future aspirations. Again, this will help him considerably in the future. Rather than making swift progress or launching into ambitious projects, the Water Tiger would do well to regard the year more as a time of consolidation, of learning and renewal. In this respect, it will prove both a significant and important time for him. In his work the Water Tiger needs to exercise both care and caution. He should remain mindful of the views of those around him as well as be willing to adapt to new and changing situations. To retain an independent or intransigent stance could leave him isolated and in some difficulty. Similarly, the Water Tiger needs to exercise restraint in his spending and deal with financial matters with care. This is not a year for taking financial risks and he would do well to avoid speculative undertakings. On a more positive note, the Water Tiger's family and friends will give him considerable pleasure over the year. Although his family life will be busy and there will be many demands placed upon his time, he will take considerable delight in the activities and successes enjoyed by those around him. Throughout the year the Water Tiger would also do well to encourage joint family projects rather than trying to do too much single-handed. He will find joint activities will give all concerned a considerable amount of satisfaction. The Water Tiger will also enjoy any travelling that he undertakes over the year, particularly to places that appeal to his adventurous nature. Generally, despite the need for care in his work and financial matters, the year will contain some enjoyable times for him. In many respects 1996 will be a year of self-discovery and the experience the Water Tiger gains will serve him splendidly for the opportunities that await him in the next few years.

This will be a mixed year for the *Wood Tiger* and while certain areas of his life will bring him pleasure, he could also face some difficulties and problems. Early in the year the Wood Tiger would do well to consider his present position and his future aspirations. He should set himself some priorities for the year and decide what he really wants to achieve. This way he will be able to set about his activities in a more purposeful and disciplined way; without any plan he could easily drift and not make the most of his many talents. In 1996 the Wood Tiger can make progress, but it does require persistence and determination on his part. He should also remain mindful of the views of those around him and if he has any worries or concerns, especially in his work, he will gain much from speaking to those with experience. In his work, however, the Wood Tiger should remain realistic in his objectives and also avoid the temptation of trying to achieve too much too soon or accomplish something before he has the necessary experience. He should also take advantage of any opportunity to extend his skills and qualifications and, if he is eligible for any courses, he should follow these up. Anything positive and constructive he can do now will do much to enhance his future prospects. The Wood Tiger also needs to exercise caution in financial matters. Many Wood Tigers will be involved in a large financial transaction over the year, particularly involving accommodation, and will need to make sure they understand all the obligations that they may be placed under. Although he is usually diligent in monetary matters, this is not a year when the Wood Tiger can afford to take risks. His family and friends will, however, give him much happiness and many will have good reason for a personal celebration. This could include an engagement, marriage or an addition to the family. Personally, the year will contain some happy and memorable moments. The Wood Tiger's social life will be active and over the year he will extend his circle of acquaintances quite considerably. He will also obtain much pleasure from both the travelling that he undertakes and from his hobbies and interests. However, if he engages in any hazardous activity, particularly when tackling DIY projects, he should make sure he follows all the precautions necessary. Throughout the year he would do well to remember the maxim 'It is better to be safe than sorry.' Although not all his activities may proceed as smoothly or as rapidly as he may like, the Wood Tiger will gain much valuable experience over the year as well as enjoying some times of great personal happiness.

This will be a reasonable year for the *Fire Tiger*. Throughout the year he will need to set about his activities at a steady pace and with a certain amount of caution. Despite his good intentions and ambitious nature, this is not a year when he can afford to rush his plans or take risks. Fortunately, though, those around him will be most supportive, and if he has any doubts over any matter, he would do well to seek their advice and opinions. He will be both reassured and comforted by the advice he is given. The Fire Tiger could also spend a considerable amount of his spare time on property matters; this could involve him in a move or in carrying out some improvements. In either case he will be well pleased with the finished result. However, if he does move or carry out DIY work, he needs to be particularly careful when lifting heavy objects. A slip or strain could cause him much discomfort and he should avoid taking any unnecessary risks. The Fire Tiger will, however, obtain considerable satisfaction from his hobbies in 1996 and he would do well to further his interests over the year. He could find a special skill he has will be much appreciated by others and could even prove remunerative for him. The Fire Tiger will also thoroughly enjoy the several journeys that he takes, particularly if they allow him to meet up with relations or long-standing friends. The Fire Tiger's domestic life will also bring him much joy and he will take considerable delight in the activities and progress of those close to him. On a more cautionary note, he does need to deal with any important paperwork he receives with great care, particularly any official forms he has to complete. If there is something he does not understand he would do well to check rather than take a risk. An oversight or delay could take the Fire Tiger some time to sort out. Similarly, he needs to be careful with financial matters and would do well to keep a close watch over his expenditure. This is not a year when he can be too indulgent in his spending. Those Fire Tigers in education will make pleasing progress over the year, although if they do have any worries, particularly over academic matters, they would do well to confide in others rather than keep their concern to themselves. In many cases they could find they have been worrying unnecessarily. Generally, provided the Fire Tiger sets about his activities with care, this is a year in which he can make steady progress.

This will be a varied year for the *Earth Tiger*. Several changes will take place – some of his own making, some unexpected – but while they will give him times of uncertainty, the events of the year will generally move in his favour. When facing change, especially if it involves his work, the Fire Tiger should be prepared to be flexible and willing to adapt to new situations. Sometimes this may not be easy, but to remain intransigent could undermine his position and the goodwill he has established over recent years. In 1996 the Earth Tiger should not be resistant to changes but view them as new opportunities and challenges for him. Some Earth Tigers will be given wider responsibilities in their work, while others may consider retiring or transferring to another position. However, in all that happens, 1996 will bring new opportunities for the Earth Tiger, opportunities that might not have been available before – and with his skills, talents and determined nature, he will be certain to make the most of them. In times of uncertainty the Earth Tiger would also do well to discuss his concerns with his family and friends; he will benefit from the advice and support he is given. His family life in particular is likely to bring him much pleasure and many Earth Tigers will be involved in some memorable family and social gatherings over the year. The summer months in particular will be a busy and eventful time. The Earth Tiger will also enjoy the travelling that he undertakes and outdoor activities, such as gardening, walking or trips in the countryside, will bring him much satisfaction. Although he should not experience any financial problems over the year, it would still be in his interests to keep a watchful eye over his level of spending. Despite the moments of uncertainty that the year will bring, there will be many occasions in 1996 that he will savour.

# FAMOUS TIGERS

Sir David Attenborough, Queen Beatrix of the Netherlands, Ludwig van Beethoven, Tony Bennett, Tom Berenger, Chuck Berry, Richard Branson, Garth Brooks, Mel Brooks, Isambard Kingdom Brunel, Agatha Christie, David Coleman, Phil Collins, Jason Connery, Alan Coren,

Gemma Craven, Tom Cruise, Paul Daniels, Emily Dickinson, David Dimbleby, Isadora Duncan, Dwight Eisenhower, Queen Elizabeth II, Roberta Flack, Frederick Forsyth, Jodie Foster, Connie Francis, Charles de Gaulle, Crystal Gayle, Susan George, Elliott Gould, Buddy Greco, Germaine Greer, Sir Alec Guinness, Harriet Harman, Lord Howe, William Hurt, Derek Jacobi, Matthew Kelly, Sarah Kennedy, Dorothy Lamour, Stan Laurel, Ian McCaskill, Karl Marx, Marilyn Monroe, Demi Moore, Eric Morecambe, Lord Owen, Marco Polo, Jonathan Porritt, John Prescott, Oliver Reed, the Princess Royal, Diana Rigg, Lionel Ritchie, Kenny Rogers, Sir Jimmy Savile, Phillip Schofield, Sir David Steel, Pamela Stephenson, Dame Joan Sutherland, Dylan Thomas, Terence Trent-D'Arby, Liv Ullman, Jon Voigt, Julie Walters, Oscar Wilde, Terry Wogan, Stevie Wonder, Natalie Wood.

29 JANUARY 1903 ～ 15 FEBRUARY 1904     *Water Rabbit*

14 FEBRUARY 1915 ～ 2 FEBRUARY 1916     *Wood Rabbit*

2 FEBRUARY 1927 ～ 22 JANUARY 1928     *Fire Rabbit*

19 FEBRUARY 1939 ～ 7 FEBRUARY 1940     *Earth Rabbit*

6 FEBRUARY 1951 ～ 26 JANUARY 1952     *Metal Rabbit*

25 JANUARY 1963 ～ 12 FEBRUARY 1964     *Water Rabbit*

11 FEBRUARY 1975 ～ 30 JANUARY 1976     *Wood Rabbit*

29 JANUARY 1987 ～ 16 FEBRUARY 1988     *Fire Rabbit*

# THE
# RABBIT

# THE PERSONALITY OF THE RABBIT

> Wondrous is the strength of cheerfulness, and its power
> of endurance – the cheerful man will do more in the same
> time, will do it better, will persevere in it longer than the
> sad or sullen.
>
> – *Thomas Carlyle: a Rabbit*

The Rabbit is born under the signs of virtue and prudence.
He is intelligent, well-mannered and prefers a quiet and
peaceful existence. He dislikes any sort of unpleasantness
and will try to steer clear of arguments and disputes. He is
very much a pacifist and tends to have a calming influence
on those around him.

He has wide interests and usually has a good appreciation of the arts and the finer things in life. He also knows
how to enjoy himself and will often gravitate to the best
restaurants and night spots in town.

The Rabbit is a witty and intelligent speaker and loves
being involved in a good discussion. His views and advice
are often sought by others and he can be relied upon to be
discreet and diplomatic. He will rarely raise his voice in
anger and will even turn a blind eye to matters which
displease him just to preserve the peace. The Rabbit likes to
remain on good terms with everyone, but he can be rather
sensitive and takes any form of criticism very badly. He
will also be the first to get out of the way if he sees any
form of trouble brewing.

The Rabbit is a quiet and efficient worker and has an
extremely good memory. He is very astute in business and
financial matters, but his degree of success often depends

on the conditions that prevail. He hates being in a situation which is fraught with tension or where he has to make quick and sudden decisions. Wherever possible he will plan his various activities with the utmost care and a good deal of caution. He does not like to take risks and does not take kindly to changes. Basically, he seeks a secure, calm and stable environment, and when conditions are right he is more than happy to leave things as they are.

The Rabbit is conscientious in most of the things he does and, because of his methodical and ever-watchful nature, he can often do well in his chosen profession. He makes a good diplomat, lawyer, shopkeeper, administrator or priest and he excels in any job where he can use his superb skills as a communicator. He tends to be loyal to his employers and is respected for his integrity and honesty, but if the Rabbit ever finds himself in a position of great power he can become rather intransigent and authoritarian.

The Rabbit attaches great importance to his home and will often spend much time and money to maintain and furnish it and to fit it with all the latest comforts – the Rabbit is very much a creature of comfort! He is also something of a collector and there are many Rabbits who derive much pleasure from collecting antiques, stamps, coins, *objets d'art* or anything else which catches their eye or particularly interests them.

The female Rabbit has a friendly, caring and considerate nature, and will do all in her power to give her home a happy and loving atmosphere. She is also very sociable and enjoys holding parties and entertaining. She has a great ability to make the maximum use of her time and, although she involves herself in numerous activities, she always manages to find time to sit back and enjoy a good read or a chat. She has a great sense of humour, is very artistic and is often a talented gardener.

The Rabbit takes considerable care over his appearance and is usually smart and very well turned out. He also attaches great importance to his relations with others and matters of the heart are particularly important to him. He will rarely be short of admirers and will often have several serious romances before he settles down. The Rabbit is not the most faithful of signs, but he will find that he is especially well-suited to those born under the signs of the Goat, Snake, Pig and Ox. Due to his sociable and easy-going manner he can also get on well with the Tiger, Dragon, Horse, Monkey, Dog and another Rabbit, but will feel ill-at-ease with the Rat and Rooster as both these signs tend to speak their mind and be critical in their comments, and the Rabbit just loathes any form of criticism or unpleasantness.

The Rabbit is usually lucky in life and often has the happy knack of being in the right place at the right time. He is talented and quick-witted, but he does sometimes put pleasure before work, and wherever possible will tend to opt for the easy life. He can at times be a little reserved and suspicious of the motives of others, but generally the Rabbit will lead a long and contented life and one which – as far as possible – will be free of strife and discord.

# THE FIVE DIFFERENT TYPES OF RABBIT

In addition to the 12 signs of the Chinese zodiac, there are five elements and these have a strengthening or moderating influence on the sign. The effects of the five elements on the Rabbit are described below, together with the years in which the elements were exercising their influence. Therefore all Rabbits born in 1951 are Metal Rabbits, those born in 1903 and 1963 are Water Rabbits, and so on.

## Metal Rabbit: 1951

This Rabbit is capable, ambitious and has very definite views on what he wants to achieve in life. He can occasionally appear reserved and aloof, but this is mainly because he likes to keep his thoughts and ideas to himself. He has a very quick and alert mind and is particularly shrewd in business matters. He can also be very cunning in his actions. The Metal Rabbit has a good appreciation of the arts and likes to mix in the best circles. He usually has a small but very loyal group of friends.

## Water Rabbit: 1903, 1963

The Water Rabbit is popular, intuitive and keenly aware of the feelings of those around him. He can, however, be rather sensitive and tends to take things too much to heart. He is very precise and thorough in everything he does and has an exceedingly good memory. He tends to be quiet and at times rather withdrawn, but he expresses his ideas well and is highly regarded by his family, friends and colleagues.

## Wood Rabbit: 1915, 1975

The Wood Rabbit is likeable, easy going and very adaptable. He prefers to work in groups rather than on his own and likes to have the support and encouragement of others. He can, however, be rather reticent in expressing his views and it would be in his own interests to become a little more open and forthright and let others know how he feels on certain matters. He usually has many friends and enjoys an active social life. He is noted for his generosity.

## Fire Rabbit: 1927, 1987

The Fire Rabbit has a friendly, outgoing personality. He likes socializing and being on good terms with everyone. He is discreet and diplomatic and has a very good understanding of human nature. He is also strong-willed and provided he has the necessary backing and support he can go far in life. He does not, however, suffer adversity well and can become moody and depressed when things are not working out as he would like. The Fire Rabbit is very intuitive and there are some who are even noted for their psychic ability. The Fire Rabbit has a particularly good manner with children.

## Earth Rabbit: 1939

The Earth Rabbit is a quiet individual, but he is neverthe-less very shrewd and astute. He is realistic in his aims and is prepared to work long and hard in order to achieve his objectives. He has good business sense and is invariably lucky in financial matters. He also has a most persuasive manner and usually experiences little difficulty in getting others to fall in with his plans. He is held in very high esteem by his friends and colleagues and his views and opinions are often sought and highly valued.

# PROSPECTS FOR THE RABBIT IN 1996

The Chinese New Year starts on 19 February 1996. Until then, the old year, the Year of the Pig, is still making its presence felt.

The Year of the Pig (31 January 1995 to 18 February 1996) will have been a variable year for the Rabbit; some of the year will have gone splendidly for him, while in work and money matters he will have needed to proceed cautiously.

The remaining months of the Pig year will, however, be a generally pleasant time for the Rabbit. His family and social life in particular will be most enjoyable and he can look forward to some happy and memorable times with those around him. The Pig year is an especially fine time for the unattached Rabbit and for those who are lonely or seeking friends there will be plenty of opportunities to meet others in the closing stages of the year. Generally, on a personal level, the Pig year is often a memorable time and there will be many Rabbits who will have met their future partner over the year, got engaged, married or had some other reason for a personal celebration. The last few weeks of the Pig year will be a most enjoyable time.

The Rabbit will also obtain much pleasure from his hobbies and interests over the year, especially from any that allow him to promote and further his creative talents. If he has any opportunity to bring his skills to the attention of others, he should do so. Aspiring Rabbit artists or writers or those in the performing arts could receive some encouraging news in the closing stages of the year.

The Rabbit can also make some progress in his work at this time but should avoid taking risks or ignoring the views of others. In work matters the Pig year calls for caution. The Rabbit also needs to take care in financial affairs – while he is usually prudent in handling finance, he cannot afford to take risks and should be wary of any highly speculative ventures he hears about. The last few weeks of the Pig year can be expensive for him and all Rabbits would do well to keep a close watch over their level of expenditure at this time.

The Year of the Rat starts on 19 February and is going to be a mixed year for the Rabbit. During the year he will be able to make reasonable progress with many of his activities, but he may also have to contend with some problems and obstacles.

In his work the Rabbit can make substantial progress and for those seeking work or wishing to transfer to another position, the prospects are generally encouraging.

Many Rabbits will spot opportunities they can pursue in the early months of the year and April and May could prove particularly significant for career matters. However, while many Rabbits will make progress in their work over the year, the Rabbit still needs to exercise a certain caution in his activities. He should avoid taking unnecessary risks and should also be wary of information he receives from dubious sources. Without care he could be misled by gossip and rumours or find that others are being less than honest with him. Where important matters are concerned, if the Rabbit has any doubts, he should check the facts carefully and not necessarily believe all he is told. Fortunately, his perceptive nature will help him considerably over the year, but he does need to be on his guard.

The Rabbit would also do well to use any opportunity he gets to extend his skills and qualifications and if he is able to take any courses, even perhaps a home-study course, he should do so. He could find learning another skill both pleasurable and satisfying as well as usefully occupying some of his time. As with last year, Rabbits involved in creative matters can do well and it would be in their interests to keep promoting and furthering their work as much as they can.

The Rabbit also needs to be his usual careful self when dealing with financial matters. Again, this is not a year when he can afford to take risks and he should avoid highly speculative ventures. Similarly, where investments are concerned, he should not allow himself to be swayed by information from uncertain sources. All is not as it may appear and if he has any doubts about any financial matter, he would do well to seek a second opinion. However, while he will need to exercise care when dealing with finance, the Rabbit could be particularly fortunate in purchases that he makes over the year. By keeping alert he could make some excellent acquisitions for himself and his home, especially in the first few months of the Rat year.

The Rabbit's domestic life will bring him much pleasure and he can look forward to some most pleasant times with those around him. However, he would do well to involve his family in his various activities and be prepared to discuss any anxieties and concerns that he has. He will find that being open in this way will help lessen any burden he may feel under and he will appreciate the support he is given. He should also make sure he fully involves himself in family activities over the year and not become so preoccupied with his own concerns that he does not take as much interest in the activities of his loved ones as he should.

Also on a cautionary note, the Rabbit does need to exercise care if he undertakes any hazardous activity, particularly when moving heavy objects or using machinery. Hopefully nothing untoward will happen, but 1996 is a year for care and he would do well to take all the precautions necessary.

Similarly, the Rabbit should not neglect his own well-being. If he can take up some additional exercise, this, together with a well-balanced diet, will do much to revitalize him and leave him feeling fitter and better in himself. Anything positive that the Rabbit can do in health matters would be in his interest.

The Rabbit will lead a pleasing social life over the year and can look forward to attending several enjoyable functions and social occasions. However, he again needs to be wary of gossip and not believe all that he hears. He should also be careful about letting new acquaintances into his confidence until they have his full trust. In matters of personal relations, the Rabbit does need to be careful throughout the year.

The unattached Rabbit will generally enjoy 1996 and there will be many opportunities for romance. However, the Rabbit would do well to let any new romance develop gradually rather than rush into any commitment or build up high hopes after just a short meeting. This way he will be able to put the relationship on a firmer foundation.

Generally, 1996 will be a reasonable year for the Rabbit and there will be parts which he will very much enjoy. He will make progress in his work but he does need to exercise care in financial matters and would do well to avoid speculative or risky undertakings. He also needs to handle his relations with others with care; if not, he could find that other people let him down or abuse the confidence he has placed in them. Fortunately, though, the Rabbit is most perceptive when dealing with others and throughout the year his usual good sense and judgement will prevail.

As far as the different types of Rabbit are concerned, this will be a reasonable year for the *Metal Rabbit*. However, he does need to exercise a certain caution with his various activities and not take undue risks. This is a year for steady rather than swift progress. In his work the Metal Rabbit will continue to impress with his conscientious and methodical manner, but at all times he would do well to remain mindful of the views and opinions of his colleagues.

Also, if he has any ideas or projects he wishes to pursue, he should make sure he has the necessary support before proceeding. Throughout the year the Metal Rabbit needs to work closely with others rather than retain too much of an independent stance. Those Metal Rabbits seeking work should also remain vigilant for opportunities they can pursue, particularly in the springtime. An opening that they hear of by chance could turn into a splendid opportunity for them. The Metal Rabbit is usually most careful when dealing with financial matters, but in 1996 he does need to be vigilant. He should avoid taking unnecessary risks or committing himself to transactions without checking all the implications. Without care, an oversight could take some time to sort out. The Metal Rabbit's family life will, however, give him much pleasure and he will be particularly proud of the achievements of a younger relation. Many Metal Rabbits will also have good cause for a family celebration over the year, either involving a marriage in their family or the birth of a grandchild. As the Metal Rabbit will be kept fairly occupied over the year, particularly in work matters, he should take care not to sacrifice time with his loved ones. He should keep himself fully involved in family activities and if he does have any matters that are bothering him he should let them be known rather than keep them to himself. Many Metal Rabbits will also carry out work on their home over the year and, while the Metal Rabbit will be pleased with what he is able to accomplish, he does need to be careful if he intends to carry out anything of a hazardous nature. He may not lead as active a social life in 1996 as he has had in recent years and, as with other Rabbits, he needs to be especially careful about whom he lets into his confidence. Provided he does not take undue risks and is his usual careful self, however, this will be a pleasant year for him.

This will be a variable but important year for the *Water Rabbit*. He could have difficulty in carrying out some of his plans and ideas, and could find that he is lacking the necessary support or that conditions are against him. However, while he may face some disappointment in 1996, any difficulties that arise will help him to examine his present position and think about his future aspirations. It will be a time of self-analysis, a time for reflection and, importantly, a time for planning. For many *Water Rabbits* 1996 will be a turning-point in their lives and mark the start of a new and important phase. Admittedly, the year may bring with it some uncertainties, but events will eventually move in the Water Rabbit's favour. Over the year he will learn much about himself and his attributes, and some of the events that happen, both good and bad, will help to strengthen his resolve and motivate him. However, in all that he does, he needs to bear in mind the views of those around him and, if in doubt, should seek the advice of others. The Water Rabbit's domestic life will, however, give him considerable satisfaction and he can look forward to some most pleasant family occasions. At some point in the year, however, he may need to give some assistance to a close relation who is experiencing some difficulty. The support he is able to give will, though, be greatly valued. The Water Rabbit will lead an enjoyable social life in 1996 and will be able to widen his circle of friends and acquaintances. There will also be several opportunities for him to travel over the year, sometimes at short notice, and the journeys that he makes will prove both interesting and enjoyable for him. If possible, he should take advantage of any opportunity to visit relatives he has not seen for some time; any such visit is likely to bring all concerned much happiness. Although the year will not be without its problems and the Water Rabbit will need to proceed carefully with his various activities, there will be many times in 1996 that he will enjoy and the experience he gains will be an important stepping-stone to the better times that lie ahead. Significantly, the next few years will herald some splendid opportunities for him.

The *Wood Rabbit* has many fine skills and talents and is eager to give of his best. However, despite his well-meaning intentions, 1996 is a year for caution. He should be wary of trying to achieve too much too soon or of being over-ambitious in his objectives. If he is, he could find his plans frustrated or be disappointed. In 1996 he *can* make progress, but he should be modest in his expectations. In his work the Wood Rabbit will gain much valuable experience, but he would do well to remain flexible in his outlook and be prepared to adapt to any changing situation. Many Wood Rabbits will take on additional responsibilities over the year or move to a different type of work and while this may prove unsettling at the time, it will all be good experience – experience to build on in the future. The months of March, April and September could prove significant for career matters. The Wood Rabbit also needs to be careful with finance and should keep a close watch on his level of expenditure. He would do well to avoid risky or speculative ventures and if he has doubts over any financial transaction, he should seek additional advice. This is not a year in which he can afford to take financial risks. The Wood Rabbit will, however, greatly enjoy the travelling that he undertakes over the year and a holiday that he takes during the summer will prove especially memorable for him as well as lead to some new friendships. There will also be some delightful times with family and friends and many Wood Rabbits will have good reason to be involved in a personal celebration over the year. Those Wood Rabbits involved in education will find that the time they devote to their studies will be well rewarded and academic matters will go especially well. Anything that the Wood Rabbit can do, whether in further education or not, to enhance his skills and qualifications will be to his future good. Generally, provided he sets about his activities with care, the Wood Rabbit can make reasonable progress over the year. He will gain much useful experience and this will help his prospects considerably over the next few years.

This will be a pleasant year for the *Fire Rabbit*. In the first few months he would do well to set himself some objectives and goals to aim for. This could involve taking up a new hobby or interest, acquiring an additional skill, carrying out a project on his home or pursuing some personal aspiration. By giving himself something specific to concentrate on he will make good use of the year and be pleased with his achievements. Without any such objective, he could drift through 1996 and not have much to show for his efforts. The Fire Rabbit could also enjoy several strokes of good fortune this year – this could include receiving some money from an unexpected source or even winning a competition. His family and social life will also give him much pleasure and he can look forward to some enjoyable times with those around him. He could also extend his circle of friends and acquaintances and any Fire Rabbit who may have felt lonely or who has had some recent adversity to contend with would do well to go out more and get in contact with others. He will be pleased he has made the effort. In 1996 all Fire Rabbits will find that positive efforts will bring results. The Fire Rabbit will enjoy the travelling that he undertakes over the year and will find outings and visits to places of local interest particularly pleasurable. Generally, the year will hold some very happy times for him, although there are certain points he would do well to watch. As with all Rabbits, the Fire Rabbit should be wary about whom he lets into his confidence and if he has any doubts over information he is given, he would do well to check. Similarly, despite any good fortune he enjoys in financial matters, he should not take any unnecessary risks or get involved in highly speculative ventures. With matters of finance this is a year for caution and restraint. However, if he uses his time wisely and devotes himself to specific tasks, the Fire Rabbit will be well pleased with his accomplishments and generally this will be both a constructive and enjoyable year for him.

This will be an interesting year for the *Earth Rabbit* and while not all his activities may work out in the manner he would have liked, it will still hold several excellent opportunities for him. He should be prepared to adapt to new situations, but also remain mindful of the views and opinions of those around him. To remain intransigent or inflexible over any important matter could cause him problems and also undermine his position. The Earth Rabbit will also find that out of some of the changes that occur new openings will emerge, some of which he will find stimulating challenges. These will give him an added incentive to do well. The message for the Earth Rabbit in 1996 is: stay alert, be prepared to be flexible and remain positive. The events of the year, in the long term, can prove highly significant. The Earth Rabbit would also do well to consider taking up a new interest in 1996, something that he has never done before. Again, he will find the challenge this gives him will prove most stimulating as well as uncovering talents he never realized he had. The Earth Rabbit will be generally fortunate in money matters, but would do well to keep a close watch on his level of spending and avoid risky investments. He will thoroughly enjoy any holiday or breaks that he takes over the year and some, arranged at short notice, could prove especially memorable. His family and social life, too, will give him much pleasure. Those around him will be supportive, although if there is any domestic matter causing him disquiet, he would do well to let his feelings be known rather than keep them to himself. The Earth Rabbit will, however, find the second half of the year smoother than the first and while he may have to alter some of his plans to fit in with others, the events of 1996 will gradually turn in his favour and eventually herald the start of some new and positive trends ahead.

# FAMOUS RABBITS

Prince Albert, Lucy Arnaz, Cecil Beaton, Harry Belafonte, Ingrid Bergman, Melvyn Bragg, Gordon Brown, James Caan, Lewis Carroll, Fidel Castro, John Cleese, Confucius, Christopher Cross, Dr Jack Cunningham, Marie Curie, Kenny Dalglish, Peter Davison, Paul Eddington, Albert Einstein, George Eliot, Peter Falk, W. C. Fields, Peter Fonda, James Fox, Sir David Frost, James Galway, Cary Grant, Edvard Grieg, John Gummer, Oliver Hardy, Paul Hogan, Bob Hope, Whitney Houston, John Hurt, Chrissie Hynde, Clive James, Henry James, David Jason, Anatoli Karpov, Gary Kasparov, Michael Keaton, John Keats, Danny La Rue, Cheryl Ladd, Julian Lennon, Patrick Lichfield, Gina Lollobrigida, Robert Ludlum, Ali MacGraw, Trevor McDonald, George Michael, Roger Moore, Nanette Newman, Brigitte Nielsen, Tatum O'Neal, Christina Onassis, George Orwell, John Peel, Eva Peron, Edith Piaf, Chris Rea, John Ruskin, Ken Russell, Mort Sahl, Elisabeth Schwarzkopf, George C. Scott, Selina Scott, Sir Walter Scott, Neil Sedaka, Jane Seymour, Gillian Shephard, Georges Simenon, Neil Simon, Frank Sinatra, Dusty Springfield, Sting, Jimmy Tarbuck, Sir Denis Thatcher, J. R. R. Tolkien, Arturo Toscanini, Tina Turner, Luther Vandross, Queen Victoria, Terry Waite, Andy Warhol, Orson Welles, Walt Whitman.

| | |
|---|---|
| 16 FEBRUARY 1904 ∼ 3 FEBRUARY 1905 | *Wood Dragon* |
| 3 FEBRUARY 1916 ∼ 22 JANUARY 1917 | *Fire Dragon* |
| 23 JANUARY 1928 ∼ 9 FEBRUARY 1929 | *Earth Dragon* |
| 8 FEBRUARY 1940 ∼ 26 JANUARY 1941 | *Metal Dragon* |
| 27 JANUARY 1952 ∼ 13 FEBRUARY 1953 | *Water Dragon* |
| 13 FEBRUARY 1964 ∼ 1 FEBRUARY 1965 | *Wood Dragon* |
| 31 JANUARY 1976 ∼ 17 FEBRUARY 1977 | *Fire Dragon* |
| 17 FEBRUARY 1988 ∼ 5 FEBRUARY 1989 | *Earth Dragon* |

# THE
# DRAGON

# THE PERSONALITY OF
# THE DRAGON

Formula of my happiness: a Yes, a No, a straight line, a goal...

*— Friedrich Nietzsche: a Dragon*

The Dragon is born under the sign of luck. He is a proud and lively character and has a tremendous amount of self-confidence. He is also highly intelligent and very quick to take advantage of any opportunities that occur. He is ambitious and determined and will do well in practically anything which he attempts. He is also something of a perfectionist and will always try and maintain the high standards which he sets himself.

The Dragon does not suffer fools gladly and will be quick to criticize anyone or anything that displeases him. He can be blunt and forthright in his views and is certainly not renowned for being either tactful or diplomatic. He does, however, often take people at their word and can occasionally be rather gullible. If he ever feels that his trust has been abused or his dignity wounded he can sometimes become very bitter and it will take him a long time to forgive and forget.

The Dragon is usually very outgoing and is particularly adept at attracting attention and publicity. He enjoys being in the limelight and is often at his best when he is confronted by a difficult problem or tense situation. In some respects he is a showman and he rarely lacks an audience. His views and opinions are very highly valued and he invariably has something interesting – and sometimes controversial – to say.

He has considerable energy and is often prepared to work long and unsocial hours in order to achieve what he wants. He can, however, be rather impulsive and does not always consider the consequences of his actions. He also has a tendency to live for the moment and there is nothing that riles him more than to be kept waiting. The Dragon hates delay and can get extremely impatient and irritable over even the smallest of hold-ups.

The Dragon has an enormous faith in his abilities, but he does run the risk of becoming over-confident and unless he is careful he can sometimes make grave errors of judgement. While this may prove disastrous at the time, he does have the tenacity and ability to bounce back and pick up the pieces again.

The Dragon has such an assertive personality, so much will-power and such a desire to succeed that he will often reach the top of his chosen profession. He has considerable leadership qualities and will do well in positions where he can put his own ideas and policies into practice. He is usually successful in politics, show business, as the manager of his own department or business, and in any job which brings him into contact with the media.

The Dragon relies a tremendous amount on his own judgement and can be scornful of other people's advice. He likes to feel self-sufficient and there are many Dragons who cherish their independence to such a degree that they prefer to remain single throughout their lives. However, the Dragon will often have numerous admirers and there are many who are attracted by his flamboyant personality and striking looks. If he does marry, he will usually marry young and will find himself particularly well-suited to those born under the signs of the Snake, Rat, Monkey and Rooster. He will also find the Rabbit, Pig, Horse and Goat make ideal companions and will readily join in with many of his escapades. Two Dragons will also get on well together, as they understand each other, but the Dragon may not find things so easy with the Ox and Dog, as both will be critical of his impulsive and somewhat extrovert manner. He will also find it difficult to form an alliance with the Tiger, for the Tiger, like the Dragon, tends to speak his mind, is very strong-willed and likes to take the lead.

The female Dragon knows what she wants in life and sets about everything she does in a very determined and positive manner. No job is too small for her and she is often prepared to work extremely hard until she has secured her objective. She is immensely practical and somewhat liberated. She hates being bound by routine and petty restrictions and likes to have sufficient freedom to be able to go off and do what she wants to do. She will keep her house tidy but is not one for spending hours on house-work – there are far too many other things that she feels are more important and that she prefers to do. Like her male counterpart, she has a tendency to speak her mind.

The Dragon usually has many interests and enjoys sport and other outdoor activities. He also likes to travel and often prefers to visit places that are off the beaten track rather than head for popular tourist attractions. He has a very adventurous streak in him and providing his financial circumstances permit – and the Dragon is usually sensible with his money – he will travel considerable distances during his lifetime.

The Dragon is a very flamboyant character and while he can be demanding of others and in his early years rather precocious, he will have many friends and will nearly always be the centre of attention. He has charisma and so much confidence in himself that he can often become a source of inspiration for others. In China he is the leader of the carnival and he is also blessed with an inordinate share of luck.

# THE FIVE DIFFERENT TYPES OF DRAGON

In addition to the 12 signs of the Chinese zodiac, there are five elements and these have a strengthening or moderating influence on the sign. The effects of the five elements on the Dragon are described below, together with the years in which the elements were exercising their influence. Therefore all Dragons born in 1940 are Metal Dragons, those born in 1952 are Water Dragons, and so on.

## Metal Dragon: 1940
This Dragon is very strong-willed and has a particularly forceful personality. He is energetic, ambitious and tries to be scrupulous in his dealings with others. He can also be blunt and to the point and usually has no hesitation in speaking his mind. If people disagree with him, or are not prepared to co-operate, he is more than happy to go his own way. The Metal Dragon usually has very high moral

values and is held in great esteem by his friends and colleagues.

## Water Dragon: 1952

This Dragon is friendly, easy-going and intelligent. He is quick-witted and rarely lets an opportunity slip by. However, he is not as impatient as some of the other types of Dragon and is more prepared to wait for results rather than expect everything to happen that moment. He has an understanding nature and is prepared to share his ideas and co-operate with others. His main failing, though, is a tendency to jump from one thing to another rather than concentrate on the job in hand. He has a good sense of humour and is an effective speaker.

## Wood Dragon: 1904, 1964

The Wood Dragon is practical, imaginative and inquisitive. He loves delving into all manner of subjects and can quite often come up with some highly original ideas. He is a thinker and a doer and has sufficient drive and commitment to put many of his ideas into practice. He is more diplomatic than some of the other types of Dragon and has a good sense of humour. He is very astute in business matters and can also be most generous.

## Fire Dragon: 1916, 1976

This Dragon is ambitious, articulate and has a tremendous desire to succeed. He is a hard and conscientious worker and is often admired for his integrity and forthright nature. He is very strong-willed and has considerable leadership qualities. He can, however, rely a bit too much on his own judgement and fail to take into account the views and feelings of others. He can also be rather aloof and it would certainly be in his own interests to let others join in more with his various activities. The Fire Dragon usually gets much enjoyment from music, literature and the arts.

## Earth Dragon: 1928, 1988

The Earth Dragon tends to be quieter and more reflective than some of the other types of Dragon. He has a wide variety of interests and is keenly aware of what is going on around him. He also has clear objectives and usually has no problems in obtaining support and backing for any of his ventures. He is very astute in financial matters and is often able to accumulate considerable wealth. He is a good organizer, although he can at times be rather bureaucratic and fussy. He mixes well with others and has a large circle of friends.

# PROSPECTS FOR THE DRAGON IN 1996

The Chinese New Year starts on 19 February 1996. Until then, the old year, the Year of the Pig, is still making its presence felt.

The Year of the Pig (31 January 1995 to 18 February 1996) will have been a generally pleasant year for the Dragon and the closing stages will be both a busy and significant time for him. In what remains of the Pig year the Dragon should continue to set about his activities in his usual conscientious way. In his work he can accomplish much, but he does need to remain mindful of the views of others. He should also make every effort to keep his forthright nature in check and if he does find himself in any fraught or difficult situation he would do well to think before he speaks. A hasty remark could undo some of the good the Dragon has achieved over the year!

At this time the Dragon should also try to complete any outstanding matters or projects that he has. This can include his work, personal correspondence or projects around his house. With a concerted effort he will be delighted with what he is able to accomplish and it will also leave him freer to enjoy the Christmas and New Year holidays.

The Dragon will lead an active and pleasant social life towards the end of the year, although he would do well to listen carefully to any advice that those around him may give. What he is told could prove most helpful to him in the year ahead. Also, if he has experienced any strains and tensions in a relationship with someone over the year, he would do well to use any opportunity he gets to resolve any differences that remain. He could find that a conciliatory and understanding approach will do much to ease any problem. Again, by applying himself to a specific task, the Dragon can accomplish much.

There will also be several opportunities for the Dragon to travel at this time and the journeys he goes on will prove both interesting and highly pleasurable for him.

December 1995 and January 1996 will be two active and enjoyable months for the Dragon and if, during these months, he can think about his future aims and plans, he will find that this will do much to assist his progress in the new Chinese year.

The Year of the Rat starts on 19 February and will be an excellent year for the Dragon. Throughout he will make good progress with many of his activities as well as enjoying some splendid times with his family and friends.

To take advantage of the aspects that prevail, however, the Dragon would do well to give himself some priorities for the year and have some specific objectives to go after. By concentrating his efforts, he can achieve much. In his work there will be significant opportunities to pursue and throughout the year he should remain alert for ways in which he can advance his present position. If he is seeking promotion or wishing to change to a different type of work, he should follow up any openings that he sees. The first half of the year is particularly favourable for work activities.

Similarly, if the Dragon has any ideas or projects he wishes to pursue, this would be a good year to put them in motion. Those around him will be generally supportive and he will find that most of what he does in 1996 will be well received. In the Rat year the Dragon needs to give of his best and use his talents to the fullest.

Those Dragons seeking work should also follow up any opportunities that they see. Many will find their persistence rewarded and could find that one opportunity – no matter how small – will lead to another. The Dragon would also do well to consider types of work which he has not undertaken before. He could find the challenge this gives him most satisfying as well as usefully extending his experience.

In addition to making progress in his work the Dragon can look forward to a significant improvement in his financial situation. He will also be pleased with some purchases that he makes – both for himself and for his home – but he would do well to save or invest any spare money he does not immediately need. In future years he could be particularly grateful for the sum he has put aside.

The Dragon's social life will be generally active and give him much pleasure and, for the unattached Dragon, the aspects for new friendships, romance, getting engaged or marrying are excellent. Socially, this will be a splendid year and the Dragon can look forward to having some memorable times with his friends. For any Dragons who may have felt lonely or had to contend with some personal misfortune, this would be a good year to go out more and build up a new and fresh social life. They could find that joining a local club or society will not only widen their circle of friends but also give them another valuable interest. Again, positive action will lead to pleasing results.

With his active nature, the Dragon will also delight in

outdoor pursuits over the year and for those Dragons who enjoy travelling, follow sport or being out-of-doors, the year will hold many satisfying moments.

The Dragon's family life will also bring him much happiness. Throughout the year his family will be most supportive and give him much encouragement for his various activities. However, although the Dragon does like to follow his own judgement and relies a great deal on his intuition, he would do well to listen to his family's views and advice. They do speak with his best interests at heart and also sometimes with the benefit of experience.

The Dragon is likely to carry out several projects on his home and garden over the year and while these may take him longer than he anticipated, he will be pleased with what he is able to accomplish. Alternatively, some Dragons will choose to move over the year and while this will prove disruptive and time consuming, the Dragon will delight in his new location and in the change and opportunities a different area will bring.

All Dragons could also benefit from taking up a new interest over the year, preferably one which would give them a change from their usual daytime activities. They could find that this will turn into a valuable source of relaxation as well as provide them with many hours of pleasure.

The Rat year is one of the best years for the Dragon and in almost all areas of his life he will make pleasing gains and obtain much satisfaction. There will be opportunities for advancement in his career, a significant improvement in financial matters and a splendid social and domestic life. Also, for the unattached Dragon, this is an auspicious year for romance. But, to maximize these trends, the Dragon needs to remain positive and committed to his goals and aspirations. The trends may be favourable, but the Dragon does need to act and take full advantage of the opportunities that the year will bring.

As far as the different types of Dragon are concerned, 1996 will be a significant year for the *Metal Dragon*. At the start of the year he should give some thought to what he wishes to accomplish and then set out to pursue his goals. By giving himself priorities and setting about his activities in a purposeful way, the Metal Dragon can achieve much. He can look forward to making excellent progress in his work and should advance any ideas that he has or follow up any opportunities for advancement that he sees. Similarly, several changes that take place over the year will open up new chances for him. While he may have some initial misgivings about some of the events, he can still benefit from them. The Metal Dragon has many fine qualities and gifts, and by giving of his best and yet being adaptable in his outlook, he can enjoy much success. He will also be fortunate in financial matters and many Metal Dragons will receive a sum of money over the year, either in the form of a gift or for some work they have carried out in the past. If the Metal Dragon can save or invest any extra money he receives, he will find it will build into a useful asset for him in years to come. The Metal Dragon will also travel quite extensively in 1996 and will thoroughly enjoy any holidays or breaks that he takes, particularly to places he has not visited before. He will lead a busy but pleasant social life and his family will give him much support for his various activities. He can look forward to being involved in some memorable family occasions. He may not always have as much time for his interests as he would like, but is still likely to carry out several projects around his home and garden over the year and these will give him much satisfaction. Generally, 1996 will be a positive and fulfilling year for the Metal Dragon and provided he sets about his activities in a purposeful way, he can accomplish much. He should, however, be prepared to be flexible in times of change and throughout the year be determined to make the most of his considerable talents.

This will be a splendid and eventful year for the *Water Dragon*. Several changes will take place which will open up new and significant opportunities for him. This particularly applies in the areas of work and accommodation. In employment matters, there will be some ideal opportunities for the Water Dragon to improve upon his present position and many Water Dragons will be given additional responsibilities or obtain more interesting and remunerative work. Throughout 1996 the Water Dragon should remain alert for openings to pursue and ways in which he can put his skills to best use. He should also advance any ideas that he has or initiate any projects that he might have been thinking about. The Year of the Rat is a time of considerable advance for him and he needs to be bold and positive in his actions. With a determined attitude, all Water Dragons can achieve much over the year. The Water Dragon will also enjoy a noticeable upturn in his financial situation and a shrewd investment he makes now could prove most successful for him. He will, however, spend much time on home matters over the year, either in moving, buying new appliances or carrying out alterations. In all cases the Water Dragon will be pleased with what he acquires or accomplishes. He can look forward to some particularly enjoyable times with his family and friends and many Water Dragons will have good cause for a family celebration in 1996, possibly the marriage of a close relation or birth of a grandchild. However, while domestically the year will contain much happiness, there could be a matter which causes the Water Dragon some concern. If so, he would do well to express his views to others rather than keep his worry to himself. Also, if any relation or friend is in difficulties, any support or advice he is able to give will be much valued. Generally, 1996 will be a fulfilling year for the Water Dragon; he will make good progress in his work and his domestic and social life will bring him much happiness. The Water Dragon has many skills and talents, and in 1996 he should make sure that he puts them to good use. A positive approach will bring him constructive and highly satisfying results.

The Year of the Rat favours enterprise, innovation and creativity, and the *Wood Dragon* is superbly placed to take full advantage of these trends. With his sharp mind, considerable skills and plentiful ideas, he will come into his own during the year. He should pursue his aims and aspirations and take advantage of the many opportunities that the year has to offer. He would do well to promote his ideas and if there is some project that he wishes to undertake, now would be an excellent year to start. Those around him will be most supportive and, with a positive and determined attitude, the Wood Dragon can accomplish much. His work is likely to be well received and he could be successful in obtaining a new and better position or be given more challenging responsibilities. Those Wood Dragons involved in the creative arts or who have creative aspirations could do particularly well. The Wood Dragon will also enjoy good fortune in financial matters and many can look forward to receiving an additional and unexpected sum of money over the year. Domestically, this will be a busy but fulfilling year for him. He will delight in the progress and success enjoyed by a close relation and can look forward to some most enjoyable times with his family. However, if at any time over the year he feels under too much pressure or is in a dilemma about a decision he has to take, he should not hesitate to ask for support. His family and friends are there to help and he will be given much useful advice by those around him. The Wood Dragon will also obtain satisfaction from some improvements that he carries out on his home over the year, but he does need to exercise care when moving heavy objects or using potentially dangerous pieces of equipment. An accidental strain or injury could mar what will otherwise be an excellent year for him. Generally, 1996 will be one of the best years that the Wood Dragon has enjoyed for a long time, and by setting about his activities in a positive and determined manner he can enjoy considerable success. The aspects are excellent and it rests with him to make the most of the positive trends that prevail.

This will be a year many *Fire Dragons* will never forget. From a personal point of view, it will be an excellent period. There will be opportunities for the Fire Dragon to make new friends and the aspects are highly favourable for romance, getting engaged and married. Some Fire Dragons could also see an addition to their family. Personally, this will be a splendid year and any Fire Dragons who may have been feeling dispirited or lonely should make every effort to go out more and get in contact with others. The Fire Dragon will also get much useful encouragement from those around him, but at all times he should remain mindful of any advice he is given. Even though he may be sure in his own mind about what he wishes to do, his family and friends often speak with the benefit of experience and there will be much wisdom in their words. In his work the Fire Dragon does, however, need to proceed with a certain care. Although he is ambitious and eager to do well, he must be realistic in his expectations. He cannot make the great strides he wishes without first obtaining the necessary experience. However, progress is still possible and throughout the year the Fire Dragon will greatly impress others with his determined and conscientious manner. He should actively pursue any opportunities that he sees as well as take advantage of any chance he gets to widen his experience. The months of April, May and June could be particularly significant for employment opportunities. The Fire Dragon will also see an improvement in his financial position over the year, although he does still need to watch his level of expenditure. Without care and a certain restraint, he could find his outgoings are considerably more than he anticipated. Any Fire Dragon who changes his accommodation in 1996 will be well pleased with his new home and will spend many a happy hour converting it to his requirements. Domestically, personally and in his work, the year will bring the Fire Dragon many satisfying moments, and it will be both a constructive and highly pleasurable year for him.

This will be a positive year for the *Earth Dragon*. However, to make the best use of the trends that prevail, he should give some thought to what he wishes to accomplish over the next 12 months. This could concern travel, home projects or taking up a new interest or skill. By giving himself some objectives to aim for he will feel stimulated by the challenge and this will help him to make effective use of his time. The Rat year does particularly favour creative pursuits and a hobby such as writing, photography, painting or music could prove most pleasurable. There will also be several opportunities for the Earth Dragon to travel over the year, sometimes at short notice. The journeys that he goes on will prove most interesting, especially any taken in the first part of the year. The Earth Dragon's domestic and social life will also give him much pleasure and he can look forward to some enjoyable times with those around him. Generally, most of his activities will go well, but he does need to exercise care when moving heavy objects; a strain could result in considerable discomfort. Also he does need to deal with important forms and paperwork he receives with care and if there is anything which he does not fully understand, he should check. Without care, a bureaucratic problem could take some time to sort out and might distract him from more useful activities. The Earth Dragon can, however, look forward to several strokes of luck over the year and if he sees a competition that interests him, he would do well to enter. The year will hold several pleasant surprises for him and winning a competition could well be one of them! Generally, if the Earth Dragon uses his time constructively, he will be pleased with his accomplishments and, in particular, a new interest that he takes up is likely to bring him much satisfaction. This will be a year to enjoy.

## FAMOUS DRAGONS

Jenny Agutter, Moira Anderson, Jeffrey Archer, Roseanne Arnold, Joan Baez, Michael Barrymore, Count Basie, Stanley Baxter, Bill Beaumont, Saint Bernadette, Neneh Cherry, Julie Christie, Kenneth Clarke, James Coburn, Bing Crosby, Roald Dahl, Salvador Dali, Charles Darwin, Susan Dey, Neil Diamond, Matt Dillon, Christian Dior, Placido Domingo, Fats Domino, Stephen Dorrell, Faye Dunaway, Prince Edward, Adam Faith, Bruce Forsyth, Sigmund Freud, Michael Gambon, James Garner, Sir John Gielgud, Graham Greene, Che Guevara, David Hasselhoff, Sir Edward Heath, Gloria Hunniford, Joan of Arc, Grace Jones, Tom Jones, Penelope Keith, Martin Luther King, Eartha Kitt, Ian Lang, John Lennon, Abraham Lincoln, Lee Majors, Queen Margrethe II of Denmark, Brian Mawhinny, Yehudi Menuhin, François Mitterrand, Bob Monkhouse, Desmond Morris, Johnny Morris, Hosni Mubarak, Florence Nightingale, Nick Nolte, Al Pacino, Elaine Paige, Gregory Peck, Richard Pryor, Esther Rantzen, Christopher Reeve, Cliff Richard, George Bernard Shaw, Martin Sheen, Mel Smith, Ringo Starr, Princess Stephanie of Monaco, Karlheinz Stockhausen, Mr T., Shirley Temple, Anthea Turner, Raquel Welch, Mae West, Lord Wilson of Rievaulx (Harold Wilson), Frank Zappa.

| | |
|---|---|
| 4 FEBRUARY 1905 ⁓ 24 JANUARY 1906 | *Wood Snake* |
| 23 JANUARY 1917 ⁓ 10 FEBRUARY 1918 | *Fire Snake* |
| 10 FEBRUARY 1929 ⁓ 29 JANUARY 1930 | *Earth Snake* |
| 27 JANUARY 1941 ⁓ 14 FEBRUARY 1942 | *Metal Snake* |
| 14 FEBRUARY 1953 ⁓ 2 FEBRUARY 1954 | *Water Snake* |
| 2 FEBRUARY 1965 ⁓ 20 JANUARY 1966 | *Wood Snake* |
| 18 FEBRUARY 1977 ⁓ 6 FEBRUARY 1978 | *Fire Snake* |
| 6 FEBRUARY 1989 ⁓ 26 JANUARY 1990 | *Earth Snake* |

# THE

# SNAKE

# THE PERSONALITY OF THE SNAKE

Just trust yourself, then you will know how to live.
— *Johann Wolfgang von Goethe: a Snake*

The Snake is born under the sign of wisdom. He is highly intelligent and his mind is forever active. He is always planning and always looking for ways in which he can use his considerable skills. He is a deep thinker and likes to meditate and reflect.

Many times during his life he will shed one of his famous Snake skins and take up new interests or start a completely different job. The Snake enjoys a challenge and he rarely makes mistakes. He is a skilful organizer, has considerable business acumen and is usually lucky in money matters. Most Snakes are financially secure in their later years, provided they do not gamble — the Snake has the distinction of being the worst gambler in the whole of the Chinese zodiac!

The Snake generally has a calm and placid nature and prefers the quieter things in life. He does not like to be in a frenzied atmosphere and hates being hurried into making a quick decision. He also does not like interference in his affairs and tends to rely on his own judgement rather than listen to advice.

The Snake can at times appear solitary. He is quiet, reserved and sometimes has difficulty in communicating with others. He has little time for idle gossip and will certainly not suffer fools gladly. He does, however, have a good sense of humour and this is particularly appreciated in times of crisis.

The Snake is certainly not afraid of hard work and is thorough in all that he does. He is very determined and can occasionally be ruthless in order to achieve his aims. His confidence, will-power and quick thinking usually ensure his success, but should he fail it will often take a long time for him to recover. He cannot bear failure and is a very bad loser.

The Snake can also be evasive and does not willingly let people into his confidence. This secrecy and distrust can sometimes work against him and it is a trait which all Snakes should try to overcome.

Another characteristic of the Snake is his tendency to rest after any sudden or prolonged bout of activity. He burns up so much nervous energy that without proper care he can – if he is not careful – be susceptible to high blood pressure and nervous disorders.

It has sometimes been said that the Snake is a late starter in life and this is mainly because it often takes him a while to find a job with which he is genuinely happy. However, the Snake will usually do well in any position which involves research and writing and where he is given sufficient freedom to develop his own ideas and plans. He makes a good teacher, politician, personnel manager and social adviser.

The Snake chooses his friends carefully and, while he keeps a tight control over his finances, he can be particularly generous to those he likes. He will think nothing of buying expensive gifts or treating his friends or loved ones to the best theatre seats in town. In return he demands loyalty. The Snake is very possessive and he can become extremely jealous and hurt if he finds his trust has been abused.

The Snake is also renowned for his good looks and is never short of admirers. The female Snake in particular is most alluring. She has style, grace and excellent (and usually expensive) taste in clothes. A keen socializer, she is likely to have a wide range of friends and has a happy knack of impressing those who matter. She has numerous interests and her advice and opinions are often highly valued. She is generally a calm-natured person and while she involves herself in many activities, she likes to retain a certain amount of privacy in her undertakings.

The affairs of the heart are very important to the Snake and he will often have many romances before he finally settles down. He will find that he is particularly well suited to those born under the signs of the Ox, Dragon, Rabbit and Rooster. Provided he is allowed sufficient freedom to pursue his own interests, he can also build up a very satis-factory relationship with the Rat, Horse, Goat, Monkey and Dog, but he should try to steer clear of another Snake as they could very easily become jealous of each other. The Snake will also have difficulty in getting on with the honest and down-to-earth Pig, and will find the Tiger far too much of a disruptive influence on his quiet and peace-loving ways.

The Snake certainly appreciates the finer things in life. He enjoys good food and often takes a keen interest in the arts. He also enjoys reading and is invariably drawn to subjects such as philosophy, political thought, religion or the occult. He is fascinated by the unknown and his enquiring mind is always looking for answers. Some of the world's most original thinkers have been Snakes, and – although he may not readily admit it – the Snake is often psychic and relies a lot on intuition.

The Snake is certainly not the most energetic member of the Chinese zodiac. He prefers to proceed at his own pace and to do the things he wants. He is very much his own master and throughout his life he will try his hand at many things. He is something of a dabbler, but at some time – and usually when he least expects it – his hard work and efforts will be recognized and he will invariably meet with the success and the financial security which he so much desires.

# THE FIVE DIFFERENT TYPES
# OF SNAKE

In addition to the 12 signs of the Chinese zodiac, there are five elements and these have a strengthening or moderating influence on the sign. The effects of the five elements on the Snake are described below, together with the years in which the elements were exercising their influence. Therefore all Snakes born in 1941 are Metal Snakes, those born in 1953 are Water Snakes, and so on.

## Metal Snake: 1941
This Snake is quiet, confident and fiercely independent. He often prefers to work on his own and will only let a privileged few into his confidence. He is quick to spot opportunities and will set about achieving his objectives with an awesome determination. He is astute in financial matters

and will often invest his money well. He also has a liking for the finer things in life and has a good appreciation of the arts, literature, music and good food. He usually has a small group of extremely good friends and can be generous to his loved ones.

## Water Snake: 1953

This Snake has a wide variety of interests. He enjoys studying all manner of subjects and is capable of undertaking quite detailed research and becoming a specialist in his chosen area. He is highly intelligent, has a good memory, and is particularly astute when dealing with business and financial matters. He tends to be quietly spoken and a little reserved, but he does have sufficient strength of character to make his views known and attain his ambitions. He is very loyal to his family and friends.

## Wood Snake: 1905, 1965

The Wood Snake has a friendly temperament and a good understanding of human nature. He is able to communicate well with others and often has many friends and admirers. He is witty, intelligent and ambitious. He has numerous interests and prefers to live in a quiet, stable environment where he can work without too much interference. He enjoys the arts and usually derives much pleasure from collecting paintings and antiques. His advice is often very highly valued, particularly on social and domestic matters.

## Fire Snake: 1917, 1977

The Fire Snake tends to be more forceful, outgoing and energetic than some of the other types of Snake. He is ambitious, confident and never slow in voicing his opinions – and he can be very abrasive to those he does not like. He does, however, have many leadership qualities and can win the respect and support of many with his firm and resolute manner. He usually has a good sense of humour, a wide circle of friends and a very active social life. The Fire Snake is also a keen traveller.

## Earth Snake: 1929, 1989

The Earth Snake is charming, amusing and has a very amiable manner. He is conscientious and reliable in his work and approaches everything he does in a level-headed and sensible way. He can, however, tend to err on the cautious side and never likes to be hassled into making a decision. He is extremely adept in dealing with financial matters and is a shrewd investor. He has many friends and is very supportive towards the members of his family.

# PROSPECTS FOR THE SNAKE IN 1996

The Chinese New Year starts on 19 February 1996. Until then, the old year, the Year of the Pig, is still making its presence felt.

The Year of the Pig (31 January 1995 to 18 February 1996) will have been a challenging year for the Snake and in what remains of it he will need to exercise much care. He should avoid taking unnecessary risks and be careful when dealing with important matters. If he has any doubts or is in a dilemma about what action he should take, he would do well to seek sound and reliable advice.

Similarly, in his work, the Snake needs to proceed cautiously and pay close attention to all that is going on around him. The Pig year is not a year when he can afford to go it alone or act too independently of others. However, those Snakes whose work or interests are of a creative nature could enjoy some success at this time and would do well to use any opportunity they have to promote their talents. Creative activities are strongly favoured both in Pig and Rat years.

The Snake should also make sure that he involves himself fully in family activities as well as setting some time aside for recreational pursuits. Sometimes he can get so preoccupied in his own concerns that he does not take as much notice of others as he should and this could lead to strains with those around him. It is a point all Snakes would do well to watch and if the Snake has experienced any difficulties in any of his relationships recently, he should use any opportunity he gets in the closing stages of the year to resolve any outstanding differences.

Although the Pig year may not have been the easiest of years for the Snake, it can still prove an important one. In what remains of it, the Snake would do well to reflect on his present position and give some thought to his future, particularly to what he would like to achieve in the next few years. In this he will find it helpful to discuss his ideas with those around him and also speak to those with experience. At several times during the Snake's life, he tends to shed one of his skins and start something new. The Pig year could be one of these years. Its events could well cause him to change direction and embark on something new. For many Snakes, the Pig year can be an important and significant turning-point.

The Year of the Rat starts on 19 February and is going to be an eventful year for the Snake. He can make considerable progress in many of his activities and, while not all that happens may be entirely to his liking, he will still be pleased with what he is able to accomplish.

The Snake generally likes to plan his activities and is not one who cares to act without much careful thought. However, several times during the year he will find himself in a situation where he will need to take decisions quickly and adapt to changing situations. This particularly applies to his work. In 1996 several unexpected opportunities will occur and the Snake will need to act quickly if he is to take advantage of them. If not, he could miss some excellent chances and regret what might have been. Throughout the year, particularly in the early months of 1996, he needs to remain alert to all that is going on and pursue any openings that he sees. Similarly, he should make every effort to promote both his work and his ideas. Sometimes the Snake undermines his talents by hiding behind his placid exterior – in 1996 he needs to be far more assertive. For the bold and enterprising Snake the Rat year can be a year of positive progress.

Over the year many Snakes will be given more rewarding responsibilities or be successful in gaining a new and more challenging position. Those Snakes seeking work should remain alert for any openings to pursue and many could find their persistence rewarded, often at a time when they least expect it.

As with the previous year, 1996 very much favours creative and innovative activities and, with his diverse talents and original mind, the Snake is well placed to take advantage of these trends. Any Snake who has creative aspirations should promote his talents as much as he can.

The Snake will also enjoy an improvement in his financial situation and those who may have been experiencing financial problems will find that these will ease as the year progresses. The Snake would do well, however, to keep an eye over his expenditure and try not to succumb to too many expensive whims! Although usually careful in financial matters, he can sometimes be indulgent and he should think twice before purchasing expensive items on the spur of the moment. If not, he could later find himself regretting his purchase or find that he has been involved in more expense than was necessary. The Snake will, however, enjoy some success in investments that he makes and provided he steers clear of anything too speculative, he can look forward to making some pleasing gains over the year.

As this will be quite an active year for the Snake –

sometimes too active for his liking! – there will be times when he will despair of all he has to do or be in a dilemma about which is the right action to take. In times of pressure and uncertainty, the Snake would do well to involve those around him and listen carefully to their views and advice. Although the Snake likes to remain his own master, he will be grateful for the support he is given. Throughout the year he will find those around him most co-operative and they will do much to help put his mind at ease.

The Snake's domestic and social life will also give him much satisfaction. In addition to the encouragement those close to him will give, he can look forward to some happy and memorable times. He will attend several highly enjoyable social functions during the year and there will be plenty of opportunities to add to his friends and extend his acquaintances. The unattached Snake in particular can look forward to a most enjoyable year and matters of the heart are well aspected, especially in the spring and summer months. In view of the demands of the year the Snake cannot, however, afford to neglect his well-being and it would be in his interests to make sure that he sets a regular time aside to rest and unwind and that he has at least one proper break over the year. Not all Snakes have the stamina of some and the Snake does need to take good care of himself. If not, the pressures and activities of the year could leave him feeling stressed and debilitated. Also, if the Snake does not have much daily exercise he could find some additional activity such as walking, swimming or cycling most beneficial for him.

Generally, most of the Snake's activities will go well. However, over the year, he must be prepared to adapt to changing situations and act quickly on any opportunities that he sees. This is not a year when the Snake can afford the luxury of planning his activities to the finest detail. It is an eventful and potentially successful year for him and he needs to move with events. In work and financial matters, he can enjoy much success and both his domestic and social life will give him considerable pleasure. The Snake has many talents – in 1996 he must use them and give of his best.

As far as the different types of Snake are concerned, 1996 will be an important year for the *Metal Snake*. This Snake is generally cautious in his attitude and likes to plan his activities with care; in 1996 he could find himself having to alter his plans and adapt to new situations. In his work, in particular, there will be several significant changes. Some Metal Snakes will see opportunities they can swiftly turn to their advantage and will move to more interesting and rewarding responsibilities, while others may change to a different position or even consider retiring. For many, this will be a year of change. The Metal Snake could find some of the events that occur unsettling; if so, he would do well to speak of his concerns and anxieties to others rather than keep them to himself. Also, if he faces problems or opposition to any of his plans, he should look for ways around the situation rather than remain intransigent. He could find that some new plans he is able to develop are better than his old ones and he could come to view some of the events of the year – unsettling though they may be – as blessings in disguise. The Metal Snake can, however, look forward to some success in financial matters and many

Metal Snakes will receive an additional and, in some cases, unexpected sum of money over the year. The Metal Snake could also enjoy some luck in a competition that he enters. His domestic and social life will give him much satisfaction and he is likely to take much pride in the achievements of a younger relation. The Metal Snake would also do well to make sure that he devotes time to his hobbies and interests over the year as well as allow himself the opportunity to regularly unwind. Some parts of the year could prove demanding and stressful for him and he does need to take good care of himself. He could find outdoor activities such as gardening, walking or just visiting the countryside both beneficial and enjoyable for him. Generally, 1996 will be a significant year for the Metal Snake and, by adapting to the changes that occur, most Metal Snakes will be able to improve on their present situation and accomplish much. But this is very much a year when the Metal Snake needs to remain alert to all that is going on and be flexible in his attitude.

In recent years the *Water Snake* may have felt dissatis-fied with his progress or thought that his efforts have not been fully recognized or appreciated. In 1996 his patience and endeavours will be rewarded. This will be a significant and important year for him and will mark an upturn in his fortunes, an upturn that will continue for several years. In 1996 the Water Snake needs to be bold and positive in his actions and be prepared to assert himself. Sometimes, because of his reticent and reserved manner, he does not make as much of himself and his talents as he should. In 1996 he must take the initiative and go after his objectives and aspirations. If it is a new job, promotion or the realization of a personal ambition that he wants, the Water Snake should act positively. With the right attitude he can make significant strides, especially in his work. The Water Snake should also follow up any opportunities that he sees as well as actively promote his ideas. Creative activities are especially well aspected and those Water Snakes whose work is of a creative nature could enjoy singular success. The Rat year will, however, be a busy and demanding year for the Water Snake and, as far as possible, he would do well to give himself priorities rather than spread his energies too widely. In addition to the favourable aspects that exist for him in his work, financial matters will also go well and many Water Snakes will enjoy a noticeable upturn in their financial situation. The Water Snake could also make some pleasing purchases over the year and by remaining alert he could find some bargains in the most unlikely of places. His domestic life will be generally busy, but will bring him much satisfaction. Throughout the year he will be active in encouraging, supporting and advising those around him and while, at some time, he may feel under pressure and despair of all he has to do, his efforts will be much appreciated. The Water Snake may not have as much time for his personal hobbies and interests as he would like, but he should always make sure he gives himself time to rest and unwind; even just a brisk walk could do him some good as well as giving him time to collect his thoughts. Generally, 1996 will be a busy but highly rewarding year for the Water Snake. He has many talents and in 1996 he would do well to put these to their fullest use. For the bold and enterprising Water Snake, this will be one of the most productive years for a long time.

This will be a positive year for the *Wood Snake*. In recent years he is likely to have gained much valuable experience as well as building up a clearer insight into his future aspirations and objectives. In 1996 he will be able to put his experience and ideas to good use. He should make every effort to promote his skills and advance any ideas that he has. Also, if he has been thinking about launching a new scheme or project, now would be an ideal time to do so. This will be a year of considerable progress for the Wood Snake and he should make the most of his many talents and abilities. In his work he should pursue any opportunities that he sees but also be adventurous in his outlook. If he is currently dissatisfied with what he is doing or would like new and more stimulating challenges, he should consider transferring to something else. Positive action on his part will ultimately lead to significant changes. The Wood Snake will also enjoy an improvement in his financial situation in 1996, although he will be involved in some expense connected with his property, especially as he is likely to carry out several DIY and home improvements over the year. The Wood Snake's domestic life will be demanding but satisfying. He will delight in the progress and activities of those around him, but there could still be a domestic matter which arises early in the year that gives him cause for concern. In such a situation, the Wood Snake should be prepared to speak of his worries rather than keep them to himself. Also, if someone close to him does have a problem or difficulty to deal with, the support and assistance he is able to give will do much good and be appreciated more than he may realize at the time. The Wood Snake will lead a pleasant social life in 1996 and, while he may not travel too far over the year, the journeys and holidays that he does take will prove most enjoyable and will go well for him. Generally, 1996 will be an active and pleasing year for the Wood Snake and, by giving of his best, promoting his talents and pursuing any opportunities that he sees, he can make excellent progress. The aspects for the Wood Snake are most encouraging and it rests with him to take advantage of these positive trends.

This will be a fulfilling year for the *Fire Snake*. Many Fire Snakes who are unattached will meet their partner over the year, or get engaged or married, making this a most memorable year for them. Romantic matters are well aspected throughout 1996 and those Fire Snakes seeking friends or romance should take advantage of the many social opportunities available to them. The Fire Snake can also look forward to making significant progress in his work. Over the year several unexpected events could cause him to review his situation and alter some of his plans, but by being adaptable in his outlook, the Fire Snake can benefit from some of the new situations that arise. Remaining too intransigent or set in his ways could, however, undermine his progress. In his work the Fire Snake should actively pursue any opportunities that he sees as well as aim to widen his experience. If he is seeking work or is currently in a position he does not like, he should persistently follow up any openings – his determination will be rewarded, and May, September and November could be significant months for career matters. The Fire Snake will also enjoy some luck in financial affairs and those who have been experiencing financial problems will find their situation eased as the year progresses.

However, the Fire Snake would still do well to keep a close watch over his level of expenditure and try not to stretch his resources too far. If he is involved in any large purchases over the year he does need to make sure he budgets accordingly and is aware of all the implications he may be placed under. Financial matters will generally go well, but he does need to exercise care. The Fire Snake will thoroughly enjoy any travel that he undertakes in 1996 and for those who are keen on learning a foreign language or who wish to widen their experience, this would be a good year to consider working abroad or embarking on long trips. The Fire Snake will find outdoor activities particularly satisfying and those with sporting aspirations could enjoy some success. Generally, 1996 will be an enjoyable and satisfying year for the Fire Snake and by being both flexible and persistent in his activities he will make good progress. On a personal level the year will bring him much happiness.

This will be an active and enjoyable year for the *Earth Snake*. His domestic and social life will both give him much pleasure and he will have several opportunities to add to his already wide circle of friends and acquaintances. He will also take much delight in family activities over the year and can look forward to some pleasant and memorable times with those around him. Travel is also well aspected and a holiday that he takes in the early summer could prove to be one of the best he has had for a long time. He should also take advantage of any opportunity he gets to meet up with some friends or relations he has not seen for some time; such a meeting will prove most enjoyable for all concerned. His hobbies and interests too will give him considerable satisfaction, especially if he is able to contact those who share them. This will also be a favourable year for financial matters and the Earth Snake could receive an additional sum of money over the year, either as a gift or as the fruition of an investment. Also, while he is not usually extravagant in his spending, if he wants specific items for himself or his home, he could be fortunate in making some excellent purchases at most advantageous prices. On a more cautionary note, however, the Earth Snake does need to deal with important correspondence and official documents with great care. A mistake or oversight could take some time to sort out. Generally, however, most of the Earth Snake's activities will go well for him. His family and friends will bring him much pleasure, his interests satisfaction and, in many respects, this will be a year that he will have every reason to enjoy.

# FAMOUS SNAKES

Muhammad Ali, Ann-Margret, Yasser Arafat, Paddy Ashdown, Edouard Balladur, Ronnie Barker, Kim Basinger, Benazir Bhutto, Tony Blair, William Blake, Heinrich Böll, Betty Boothroyd, Brahms, Pierce Brosnan, Chubby Checker, Tom Conti, Randy Crawford, Jim Davidson, Bob Dylan, Stefan Edberg, Elgar, Sir Alexander Fleming, Henry Fonda, Mahatma Gandhi, Greta Garbo, Art Garfunkel, J. Paul Getty, Dizzy Gillespie, W. E. Gladstone, Goethe, Princess Grace of Monaco, Bob Hawke, Stephen Hawking, Nigel Hawthorne, Denis Healey, Audrey Hepburn, Jack Higgins, Paul Hogan, Michael Howard, Howard Hughes,

Rev. Jesse Jackson, Derek Jameson, Griff Rhys Jones, Stacy Keach, Howard Keel, J. F. Kennedy, Carole King, James Last, Cindi Lauper, Dame Vera Lynn, Linda McCartney, Magnus Magnusson, Mao Tse-tung, Nigel Mansell, Dean Martin, Henri Matisse, Sir Patrick Mayhew, Robert Mitchum, Nasser, Bob Newhart, Mike Oldfield, Aristotle Onassis, Jacqueline Onassis, Ryan O'Neal, Dorothy Parker, Pablo Picasso, Mary Pickford, Michael Portillo, André Previn, Helen Reddy, Franklin D. Roosevelt, Mickey Rourke, Jean-Paul Sartre, Franz Schubert, Brooke Shields, Nigel Short, Paul Simon, Delia Smith, John Thaw, Dionne Warwick, Charlie Watts, Ruby Wax, Oprah Winfrey, Victoria Wood, Virginia Woolf, Susannah York.

| | |
|---|---|
| 25 JANUARY 1906 ∼ 12 FEBRUARY 1907 | *Fire Horse* |
| 11 FEBRUARY 1918 ∼ 31 JANUARY 1919 | *Earth Horse* |
| 30 JANUARY 1930 ∼ 16 FEBRUARY 1931 | *Metal Horse* |
| 15 FEBRUARY 1942 ∼ 4 FEBRUARY 1943 | *Water Horse* |
| 3 FEBRUARY 1954 ∼ 23 JANUARY 1955 | *Wood Horse* |
| 21 JANUARY 1966 ∼ 8 FEBRUARY 1967 | *Fire Horse* |
| 7 FEBRUARY 1978 ∼ 27 JANUARY 1979 | *Earth Horse* |
| 27 JANUARY 1990 ∼ 14 FEBRUARY 1991 | *Metal Horse* |

# THE

# HORSE

# THE PERSONALITY OF THE HORSE

These three things – work, will, success – fill human existence. Will opens the door to success, both brilliant and happy. Work passes these doors, and at the end of the journey success comes in to crown one's efforts.

*– Louis Pasteur: a Horse*

The Horse is born under the signs of elegance and ardour. He has a most engaging and charming manner and is usually very popular. He loves meeting people and likes attending parties and other large social gatherings.

He is a lively character and enjoys being the centre of attention. He has considerable leadership qualities and is much admired for his honest and straightforward manner. He is an eloquent and persuasive speaker and has a great love of discussion and debate. The Horse also has a particularly agile mind and can assimilate facts remarkably quickly.

He does, however, have a fiery temper and although his outbursts are usually short-lived, he can often say things which he will later regret. He is also not particularly good at keeping secrets.

The Horse has many interests and involves himself in a wide variety of activities. He can, however, get involved in so much that he can often waste his energies on projects which he never has time to complete. He also has a tendency to change his interests rather frequently and will often get caught up with the latest craze or 'in thing' until something better or more exciting turns up.

The Horse also likes to have a certain amount of freedom and independence in the things that he does. He hates being bound by petty rules and regulations and as far as possible likes to feel that he is answerable to no one but himself. But despite this spirit of freedom, he still likes to have the support and encouragement of others in his various enterprises.

Due to his many talents and likeable nature, the Horse will often go far in life. He enjoys challenges and is a methodical and tireless worker. However, should things work against him and he fail in any of his enterprises, it will take a long time for him to recover and pick up the pieces again. Success to the Horse means everything. To fail is a disaster and a humiliation.

The Horse likes to have variety in his life and he will try his hand at many different things before he settles down to one particular job. Even then, he will probably remain alert to see whether there are any new and better opportunities for him to take up. The Horse has a restless nature and can easily get bored. He does, however, excel in any position which allows him sufficient freedom to act on his own initiative or which brings him into contact with a lot of people.

Although the Horse is not particularly bothered about accumulating great wealth, he handles his finances with care and will rarely experience any serious financial problems.

The Horse also enjoys travel and he loves visiting new and far-away places. At some stage during his life he will be tempted to live abroad for a short period of time and due to his adaptable nature he will find that he will fit in well wherever he goes.

The Horse pays a great deal of attention to his appearance and usually likes to wear smart, colourful and rather distinctive clothes. He is very attractive to the opposite sex and will often have many romances before he settles down. He is loyal and protective to his partner, but, despite his family commitments, still likes to retain a certain measure of independence and have the freedom to carry on with his own interests and hobbies. He will find that he is especially well-suited to those born under the signs of the Tiger, Goat, Rooster and Dog. The Horse can also get on well with the Rabbit, Dragon, Snake, Pig and another Horse, but he will find the Ox too serious and intolerant for his liking. The Horse will also have difficulty in getting on with the Monkey and the Rat – the Monkey is very inquisitive and the Rat seeks security and both will resent the Horse's rather independent ways.

The female Horse is usually most attractive and has a friendly, outgoing personality. She is highly intelligent, has many interests and is alert to everything that is going on around her. She particularly enjoys outdoor pursuits and often likes to take part in sport and keep-fit activities. She also enjoys travel, literature and the arts, and is a very good conversationalist.

Although the Horse can be stubborn and rather self-centred, he does have a considerate nature and is often willing to help others. He has a good sense of humour and will usually make a favourable impression wherever he goes. Provided he can curb his slightly restless nature and keep a tight control over his temper, the Horse will go through life making friends, taking part in a multitude of different activities and generally achieving many of his objectives. His life will rarely be dull.

# THE FIVE DIFFERENT TYPES OF HORSE

In addition to the 12 signs of the Chinese zodiac, there are five elements, and these have a strengthening or moderating influence on the sign. The effects of the five elements on the Horse are described below, together with the years in which the elements were exercising their influence. Therefore all Horses born in 1930 and 1990 are Metal Horses, those born in 1942 are Water Horses and so on.

## Metal Horse: 1930, 1990

This Horse is bold, confident and forthright. He is ambitious and also a great innovator. He loves challenges and takes great delight in sorting out complicated problems. He likes to have a certain amount of independence in the things that he does and resents any outside interference. The Metal Horse has charm and a certain charisma, but he can also be very stubborn and rather impulsive. He usually has many friends and enjoys an active social life.

## Water Horse: 1942

The Water Horse has a friendly nature, a good sense of humour, and is able to talk intelligently on a wide range of topics. He is astute in business matters and quick to take advantage of any opportunities that arise. He does, however, have a tendency to get easily distracted and can change his interests – and indeed his mind – rather frequently, and this can sometimes work to his detriment.

He is nevertheless very talented and can often go far in life. He pays a great deal of attention to his appearance and is usually smart and well turned out. He loves to travel and also enjoys sport and other outdoor activities.

## Wood Horse: 1894, 1954

The Wood Horse has a most agreeable and amiable nature. He communicates well with others and, like the Water Horse, is able to talk intelligently on many different subjects. He is a hard and conscientious worker and is held in high esteem by his friends and colleagues. His opinions and views are often sought and, given his imaginative nature, he can quite often come up with some very original and practical ideas. He is usually widely read and likes to lead a busy social life. He can also be most generous and often holds high moral viewpoints.

## Fire Horse: 1906, 1966

The element of Fire combined with the temperament of the Horse creates one of the most powerful forces in the Chinese zodiac. The Fire Horse is destined to lead an exciting and eventful life and to make his mark in his chosen profession. He has a forceful personality and his intelligence and resolute manner bring him the support and admiration of many. He loves action and excitement and his life will rarely be quiet. He can, however, be rather blunt and forthright in his views and does not take kindly to interference in his own affairs or to obeying orders. He is a flamboyant character, has a good sense of humour and will lead a very active social life.

## Earth Horse: 1918, 1978

This Horse is considerate and caring. He is more cautious than some of the other types of Horse, but he is wise, perceptive and extremely capable. Although he can be rather indecisive at times, he has considerable business acumen and is very astute in financial matters. He has a quiet, friendly nature and is well thought of by his family and friends.

# PROSPECTS FOR THE HORSE IN 1996

The Chinese New Year starts on 19 February 1996. Until then, the old year, the Year of the Pig, is still making its presence felt.

The Year of the Pig (31 January 1995 to 18 February 1996) will have been a mixed year for the Horse. In some areas of his life his activities will have gone well, but in others he could have experienced problems and delays. This pattern is likely to continue until the end of the Pig year.

The Horse can, however, look forward to making progress in his work and should not hesitate to promote his ideas or follow up any opportunities that he sees. With persistence and hard work, he can achieve much in the closing stages of the year, with December and January being particularly favoured months for career matters. The Horse will also be fortunate in financial matters at this time, although he would do well to exercise a certain restraint in his spending. A major spending spree could quickly deplete any surplus he has built up.

The Horse's domestic and social life will, however, give him much pleasure and he will find himself much in demand with both his family and friends. He can look forward to attending several enjoyable social functions at this time as well as adding to his already large number of acquaintances. It will also be a happy time for the single Horse and romance is well aspected.

However, while his work and social life will go well, there are certain areas that the Horse will need to watch. This particularly applies to property matters. If the Horse intends to move or carry out projects on his home, he does need to keep a close watch on all the costs and implications. Pig years do not favour property matters for the Horse and care is needed.

Similarly, the Horse needs to remain mindful of his own well-being. Although he usually has a robust constitution, the Pig year will have been a busy time for him and he does need to give himself the opportunity to relax and restore lost energy. To drive himself too hard or 'burn the candle at both ends' could leave him feeling exhausted and certainly not enjoying life as much as he could. As the Pig year draws to a close, the Horse would do well to put some time aside just to enjoy himself and give himself a well-deserved rest. With all he has done in the Pig year, he deserves it!

The Year of the Rat starts on 19 February. Rat years are generally not the best of years for the Horse and he could find his level of progress slow. However, although he may face some difficulties and delays, he can still emerge from the year with some important gains to his credit. In 1996 it is a case of proceeding carefully and cautiously and leaving nothing to chance. Some of the events that happen over the year will cause him to analyse his present position and reflect on his future aims and aspirations. However, he will come up with some new ideas about the direction he would like his future to take and this, together with the experience he gains, will help him prepare for the better and more favourable times that lie ahead. For the Horse, this is very much a year for learning, planning and preparation.

As the Horse has such a sociable and outgoing nature, he attaches much importance to his relations with others. However, throughout the year, he does need to exercise care in his relations with those around him. He should remain mindful of their views and not take their support for granted. Similarly, if he wishes to proceed with any significant plans, he should make sure he has the backing and support of those around him. This is not a year when the Horse can act alone and he will need to exercise restraint over his rather independent and self-willed nature. He will, in any case, find his plans and ideas will be strengthened by discussion with others and some of the advice he receives, particularly from his family, will prove invaluable as the year progresses. Also, if the Horse should have any matter which is concerning him, he would do well to seek the advice of those with experience. Again, what he is told will prove most helpful. If, however, the Horse meets with any opposition to his plans, he should examine the reasons why and look for ways round the problem. To remain intransigent or inflexible could make matters worse. As with so many aspects of his life in 1996, care and caution are very much the key words and if the Horse remembers this, he can make progress.

In his work he will gain from the experience and knowledge he obtains and sow the seeds for future advancement. Also, if he is able to add to his experience by going on courses or undertaking additional study, he will find that this will do much to enhance his prospects. Anything constructive he can do in furthering his skills or knowledge will be in his interests. Those Horses seeking work should remain persistent and determined and would also do well to investigate types of work which they may not have fully considered before. The Horse is, after all, most versatile and by undertaking a new type of work he could discover talents he did not know he had as well as usefully expanding on his experience. Persistence on his part will bring results. All Horses will, however, find the second half of the year more favourable for work matters than the first and there could be some splendid opportunities for advancement in the period from September to November.

The Horse will also need to exercise care in his spending over the year and if he enters any large transaction he should make sure he can meet any obligations he might be placed under. Where possible, he should avoid risky speculations as well as be wary of lending money. In monetary matters, the Horse does need to be on his guard.

The Horse's domestic life will, however, give him much pleasure over the year and he will greatly value the loyalty and affection of those around him. Both his family and friends will provide him with many happy times, but he does need to fully involve them in his activities and plans.

The Horse will also find that a new hobby or interest

that he takes up will provide him with much pleasure, both in this and future years. If there is a subject that has been intriguing him, such as learning a new skill, a foreign language or a musical instrument, he will find this an ideal year to enrol on a course or find out more. He will find taking up a new interest will prove most satisfying for him as well as putting some of his spare time to practical use.

The Horse will thoroughly enjoy any travelling that he undertakes over the year and would do well to make sure that he takes at least one good holiday or break in 1996. Although the Horse usually has much energy and vitality, he cannot drive himself relentlessly over the year and should ensure that he allows himself time to regularly relax and unwind. Also, if he relies a lot on quick and convenience foods, he could find that a more balanced diet will do much to improve his well-being.

Although the Horse will need to exercise care and caution in many of his activities, he can still accomplish much in 1996. He can make steady progress in his work, learn much from the experiences of the year and be in a good position to make progress in the future. This is a year for learning, for gaining experience and preparing himself for the significant progress that he will make in the next few years. The Rat year may not be the smoothest of years for him, but it can still be a valuable and constructive year.

As far as the different types of Horse are concerned, this will be a significant year for the *Metal Horse*. Over the course of the year he will give much thought to his future and some of the decisions he makes will have an important bearing on the events of the next few years. However, in making future plans – no matter what area of life they concern – the Metal Horse should weigh up all the options available to him and talk about his ideas with those close to him. On no account should he rush into any action without checking the facts and implications carefully or without having secured the support of others. With care and good common sense, the decisions and actions that the Metal Horse takes will work out favourably for him but, as with all things in 1996, he cannot take risks or disregard the views of those around him. He will, however, get much pleasure from his various hobbies and interests over the year, especially those that enable him to get out and about and allow him to meet others. And, although the Metal Horse is rarely at a loss for things to do, if he does feel like taking up another interest – ideally something totally different from his usual everyday activities – he will find that this will bring him much satisfaction. The Metal Horse will lead a pleasant social life in 1996 and could make some new and important friends during a holiday or short break that he takes during the summer months. As always, he will be much in demand with his family and throughout the year he would do well to remember that they are always keen to help him, should he have any problems. Similarly, if there is a family matter that does give him cause for concern, the Metal Horse should make his feelings known. He is much admired for his frankness and common sense and his views could do much to clear up any domestic problem that might have arisen. The Metal Horse does, however, need to exercise care in money matters over the year and should particularly check the details of any large purchase or financial commitment that he makes. Without care, he could find his outlay is considerably more than he intended. Generally, 1996 will be a constructive year for the Metal Horse and by acting in unison with others he can enjoy the year, add to his circle of friends and make some important plans for his future. From September onwards he will enjoy a noticeable upturn in his fortunes.

In recent years the *Water Horse* may have felt that he has not been making the most of his potential or found progress difficult. However, in 1996 he can begin to take heart and will be able to put any recent disappointments he may have had behind him. This year will be the start of a new and more positive phase in his life and he will begin to feel more optimistic about his future. However, this upturn in his fortunes will not be immediate – indeed, the year will still contain its fair share of challenges and problems – but the Water Horse should set about his activities with a renewed confidence, determined to make the most of his abilities. He should follow up activities that interest him and seek out opportunities in which he can better use his talents. By acting boldly, he can himself bring about the change in his fortunes. Throughout the year the Water Horse will be very much helped by the support of his family, friends and colleagues and, while he may have set ideas on what he wants to do and accomplish (as do all independent-minded Horses!), he would do well to pay careful attention to any advice he is given. He would also do well to reflect upon his future aims and aspirations. Some of the ideas that he develops could prove particularly significant in the years ahead. For many Water Horses 1996 will represent a turning-point in their lives – a year when they take some important decisions and when their patience, persistence and true worth will once more begin to be recognized. However, while this will be a significant year, the Water Horse would do well to remember that overall, Rat years can prove testing times for the Horse and in all his activities he cannot afford to take unnecessary risks. Domestically and socially, however, the year will hold some fulfilling times for him and he will also obtain much satisfaction from his various hobbies and interests. The Water Horse will also get particular delight from outdoor activities and from the travelling he undertakes over the year. The summer, in particular, will be a most pleasurable time for him.

The *Wood Horse* has many talents and abilities and in recent times he may have felt that he has not been making as much progress as he would have liked. He could have faced disappointments and delays and felt that his talents have not been fully appreciated or used. However, 1996 will mark an important turning-point in his fortunes. During the year he needs to seriously analyse his present position and consider just what it is he wishes to do with his life. If he has felt he has been drifting, marking time or not making the best use of his potential, now is the time to put this right. It is the time for the Wood Horse to think about his future and start to take positive action to improve upon his present position and to secure his goals. If it is a new job that he wants, a change of career, a move to a new location or some other objective, now is the time to plan and act. The Wood Horse should also discuss his thoughts and ideas with those around him and listen closely to their views. There will be much wisdom in what his family and friends advise him. For many Wood Horses, this will be the year in which they lay the foundation for a better and brighter future. Also, although this will be quite a demanding year for the Wood Horse, if he is able to set some time aside to add to his skills he could find this will do much to enhance his prospects. Generally, as far as career opportunities are concerned, the second half of the year will be more favourable than the first and there could be some splendid opportunities for him to pursue in September and October. As far as financial matters are concerned, the Wood Horse does need to be conservative in his spending over the year and avoid stretching his resources too far. This is not a year when he can take risks with his money or be too indulgent. He will, however, greatly enjoy the holidays and breaks that he takes during the year and socially he is likely to build up some new and important contacts. His home life will be busy and eventful and many Wood Horses will also have good reason to be involved in a family celebration over the year. Although the Wood Horse may not have events all his own way in 1996, this will still be a significant and generally satisfying year for him.

This will be a busy year for the *Fire Horse* and there will be many a time when he will despair of all he has to do. However, despite the demanding and challenging nature of the year, the Fire Horse can achieve much. Throughout the year he needs to sort out his priorities and decide what it is he most wants to accomplish. Sometimes the Fire Horse limits his progress by spreading his energies too widely – in 1996, he must resist this temptation and concentrate on his main objectives. If he is seeking a new job or promotion, he should pursue any openings available as well as taking advantage of any opportunities to broaden his experience. The year holds a lot of potential for him, but he does need to use his time wisely. He should also avoid taking any major decisions concerning his work without much careful thought – this is not a year to take hasty action or undue risks. Provided he is careful, however, he can make good progress. The Fire Horse's family life will also keep him fully occupied over the year and if he feels under too much pressure or has any matters that are concerning him, he should not hesitate to ask for help and advice. Those around him will be only too glad to assist him in any way. Both his family and social life will bring him considerable joy in 1996. The Fire Horse does, however, need to be careful in financial matters and avoid taking financial risks or stretching his resources too far. If he enters into any large transaction, he needs to make sure he can meet all the obligations he might be placed under. The Fire Horse will, however, obtain much pleasure from his hobbies and interests over the year and he will also greatly enjoy the travelling that he undertakes. Generally, 1996 will be a busy and demanding year for him and providing he concentrates his energies on just a limited range of activities, he can emerge from it with some worthy gains to his credit, ready to take advantage of the much improved trends that await him in 1997.

The *Earth Horse* has many fine qualities: he is eager, talented and also most ambitious. However, despite his noble intentions, this is a year in which he must proceed cautiously. In 1996 he needs to plan his activities carefully and give much thought to how he would like his life to develop over the next few years. Where possible, he should talk to those with experience, who can help him progress. The advice and help that the Earth Horse is given over the year will prove invaluable to him. Over the year he will also be able to add to his experience but he does need to be realistic in his objectives. To attempt too much too soon could lead to disappointment. This will be a year of steady rather than swift progress but, above all, it is a year for learning and getting experience. Those Earth Horses involved in academic work are, however, likely to do well and many will be successful in obtaining some important qualifications over the year. And anything that the Earth Horse can do, whether in education or not, to extend his skills will prove most useful to him in the future. He does, however, need to watch his level of expenditure carefully over the year and, as far as possible, avoid stretching his resources too far or borrowing large sums of money. This is not a year in which he can take unnecessary financial risks. His family and social life will, however, give him much pleasure and many Earth Horses will make some new and important friends. Romantic matters may not always go smoothly, however, and the Earth Horse should be wary of entering into any commitment after only a short time. He will find it better to allow any new friendship to develop over a longer period and thereby put it on a better and more solid foundation. As with most things in 1996, the Earth Horse needs to proceed carefully and cautiously. Travel is, however, well aspected and any holidays or breaks he goes on will prove most pleasurable for him and do him much good. Providing the Earth Horse sets about his activities sensibly and with care, 1996 can prove a significant year for him. For many Earth Horses it will be a time which will help them to decide the direction of their life for the next few years. With their capable nature, most will decide wisely.

# FAMOUS HORSES

Jonathan Aitken, Neil Armstrong, Rowan Atkinson, Cheryl Baker, Margaret Beckett, Samuel Beckett, Ingmar Bergman, Leonard Bernstein, Sir John Betjeman, Karen Black, Helena Bonham-Carter, Leonid Brezhnev, Ray Charles, Chopin, Sean Connery, Billy Connolly, Catherine Cookson, Ronnie Corbett, Elvis Costello, Kevin Costner, Michael Crichton, James Dean, Les Dennis, Anne Diamond, Kirk Douglas, Robert Duvall, Clint Eastwood, Thomas Alva Edison, Britt Ekland, Chris Evans, Linda Evans, Chris Evert, Ella Fitzgerald, Harrison Ford, Aretha Franklin, Sir Bob Geldof, Billy Graham, Sally Gunnell, Gene Hackman, Susan Hampshire, Rolf Harris, Rita Hayworth, Jimmy Hendrix, Ted Hughes, David Hunt, Douglas Hurd, Janet Jackson, Nikita Khrushchev, Robert Kilroy-Silk, Neil Kinnock, Dr Helmut Kohl, Lenin, Annie Lennox, Desmond Lynam, Paul McCartney, Harold Macmillan, Nelson Mandela, Princess Margaret, Curtis Mayfield, Spike Milligan, Ben Murphy, Sir Isaac Newton, Louis Pasteur, Harold Pinter, Stephanie Powers, J. B. Priestley, Puccini, Claire Rayner, Rembrandt, Ruth Rendell, Jean Renoir, Theodore Roosevelt, Helena Rubenstein, Anwar Sadat, Peter Sissons, Lord Snowdon,

Alexander Solzhenitsyn, Barbra Streisand, Kiefer Sutherland, Patrick Swayze, John Travolta, Kathleen Turner, Mike Tyson, Vivaldi, Robert Wagner, Billy Wilder, Andy Williams, the Duke of Windsor, Tammy Wynette, Boris Yeltsin, Michael York.

| | |
|---|---|
| 13 FEBRUARY 1907 ∼ 1 FEBRUARY 1908 | *Fire Goat* |
| 1 FEBRUARY 1919 ∼ 19 FEBRUARY 1920 | *Earth Goat* |
| 17 FEBRUARY 1931 ∼ 5 FEBRUARY 1932 | *Metal Goat* |
| 5 FEBRUARY 1943 ∼ 24 JANUARY 1944 | *Water Goat* |
| 24 JANUARY 1955 ∼ 11 FEBRUARY 1956 | *Wood Goat* |
| 9 FEBRUARY 1967 ∼ 29 JANUARY 1968 | *Fire Goat* |
| 28 JANUARY 1979 ∼ 15 FEBRUARY 1980 | *Earth Goat* |
| 15 FEBRUARY 1991 ∼ 3 FEBRUARY 1992 | *Metal Goat* |

# THE
# GOAT

# THE PERSONALITY OF THE GOAT

The real voyage of discovery consists not in seeking new landscapes, but in having new eyes.

*– Marcel Proust: a Goat*

The Goat is born under the sign of art. He is imaginative, creative and has a good appreciation of the finer things in life. He has an easy-going nature and prefers to live in a relaxed and pressure-free environment. He hates any sort of discord or unpleasantness and does not like to be bound by a strict routine or rigid timetable. The Goat is not one to be hurried against his will but, despite his seemingly relaxed approach to life, he is something of a perfectionist and when he starts work on a project he is certain to give of his best.

The Goat usually prefers to work in a team rather than on his own. He likes to have the support and encouragement of others and if left to deal with matters on his own he can get very worried and tends to view things rather pessimistically. Wherever possible the Goat will leave major decision-making to others while he concentrates on his own pursuits. If, however, he feels particularly strongly about a certain matter or has to defend his position in any way, he will act with great fortitude and precision.

The Goat has a very persuasive nature and often uses his considerable charm to get his own way. He can, however, be rather hesitant about letting his true feelings be known and if he were prepared to be more forthright he would do much better as a result.

The Goat tends to have a quiet, somewhat reserved

nature but when he is in company he likes he can often become the centre of attention. He can be highly amusing, a marvellous host at parties and a superb entertainer. Whenever the spotlight falls on the Goat, his adrenalin starts to flow and he can be assured of giving a sparkling performance, particularly if he is allowed to use his creative skills in any way.

Of all the signs in the Chinese zodiac, the Goat is probably the most gifted artistically. Whether it is in the theatre, literature, music or art, he is certain to make a lasting impression. He is a born creator and is rarely happier than when occupied in some artistic pursuit. But even in this, the Goat does well to work with others rather than on his own. He needs inspiration and a guiding influence, but when he has found his true *métier*, he can often receive widespread acclaim and recognition.

In addition to his liking for the arts, the Goat is usually quite religious and often has a deep interest in nature, animals and the countryside. He is also fairly athletic and there are many Goats who have excelled in some form of sporting activity.

Although the Goat is not particularly materialistic or concerned about finance, he will find that he will usually be lucky in financial matters and will rarely be short of the necessary funds to tide himself over. He is, however, rather indulgent and tends to spend his money as soon as he receives it rather than make provision for the future.

The Goat usually leaves home when he is young but he will always maintain strong links with his parents and the other members of his family. He is also rather nostalgic and is well known for keeping mementoes of his childhood and souvenirs of places that he has visited. His home will not be particularly tidy but he knows where everything is and it will also be scrupulously clean.

Affairs of the heart are particularly important to the Goat and he will often have many romances before he finally settles down. Although he is fairly adaptable, he prefers to live in a secure and stable environment and will find that he is best suited to those born under the signs of the Tiger, Horse, Monkey, Pig and Rabbit. He can also establish a good relationship with the Dragon, Snake, Rooster and another Goat, but he may find the Ox and Dog a little too serious for his liking. Neither will he care particularly for the Rat's rather thrifty ways.

The female Goat devotes all her time and energy to the needs of her family. She has excellent taste in home furnishings and often uses her considerable artistic skills to make clothes for herself and her children. She takes great care over her appearance and can be most attractive to the opposite sex. Although she is not the most well-organized of people, her engaging manner and delightful sense of humour create a favourable impression wherever she goes. She is also a good cook and usually gets much pleasure from gardening and outdoor pursuits.

The Goat can win friends easily and people generally feel relaxed in his company. He has a kind and understanding nature and although he can occasionally be stubborn, he can, with the right support and encouragement, live a happy and very satisfying life. The more he can use his creative skills, the happier he will be.

# THE FIVE DIFFERENT TYPES OF GOAT

In addition to the 12 signs of the Chinese zodiac, there are five elements, and these have a strengthening or moderating influence on the sign. The effects of the five elements on the Goat are described below, together with the years in which the elements were exercising their influence. Therefore all Goats born in 1931 and 1991 are Metal Goats, those born in 1943 are Water Goats, and so on.

## Metal Goat: 1931, 1991

This Goat is thorough and conscientious in all that he does and is capable of doing very well in his chosen profession. Despite his confident manner, he can be a great worrier and he would find it a help to discuss his worries with others rather than keep them to himself. He is loyal to his family and employers and will have a small group of extremely good friends. He has good artistic taste and is usually highly skilled in some aspect of the arts. He is often a collector of antiques and his home will be very tastefully furnished.

## Water Goat: 1943

The Water Goat is very popular and makes friends with remarkable ease. He is good at spotting opportunities but does not always have the necessary confidence to follow them through. He likes to have security both in his home life and at work and does not take kindly to change. He is articulate, has a good sense of humour and is usually very good with children.

## Wood Goat: 1895, 1955

This Goat is generous, kind-hearted and always eager to please. He usually has a large circle of friends and involves himself in a wide variety of different activities. He has a very trusting nature but he can sometimes give in to the demands of others a little too easily and it would be in his own interests if he were to stand his ground a little more often. He is usually lucky in financial matters and, like the Water Goat, is very good with children.

## Fire Goat: 1907, 1967

This Goat usually knows what he wants in life and he often uses his considerable charm and persuasive personality in order to achieve his aims. He can sometimes let his imagination run away with him and has a tendency to ignore matters which are not to his liking. He is rather extravagant in his spending and would do well to exercise a little more care when dealing with financial matters. He has a lively personality, many friends and loves attending parties and social occasions.

## Earth Goat: 1919, 1979

This Goat has a very considerate and caring nature. He is particularly loyal to his family and friends and invariably creates a favourable impression wherever he goes. He is reliable and conscientious in his work but he finds it difficult to save and never likes to deprive himself of any little luxury which he might fancy. He has numerous interests and is often very well read. He usually gets much pleasure from following the activities of various members of his family.

# PROSPECTS FOR THE GOAT IN 1996

The Chinese New Year starts on 19 February 1996. Until then, the old year, the Year of the Pig, is still making its presence felt.

The Year of the Pig (31 January 1995 to 18 February 1996) will have been a generally favourable year for the Goat, with the latter part of the year being an especially positive time. In what remains of it, the Goat should set about his activities with verve, enthusiasm and determination. All too often he can miss out on opportunities because he does not make the most of his many abilities – he must not let this happen at the end of the Pig year! He should pursue any opportunities that he sees and go after his aims and aspirations. From October 1995 onwards, the Goat can do particularly well and it remains with him to use and promote his talents wisely. With a determined and optimistic attitude, much can be achieved, particularly in his work. The Goat will also find that those around him will look favourably on his undertakings and what he accomplishes towards the end of the Pig year will help him considerably in the next Chinese year.

The Goat can also look forward to some pleasing times with his family and friends at this time. His home life over the Pig year is likely to have been busy but enjoyable and as the year closes he will find himself in ever-increasing demand with his family and friends. Domestically and socially, this will be a happy and fulfilling time for him. The unattached Goat, in particular, will have good reason to remember the Pig year and the prospects for romance and for making new friends remain excellent.

On a more cautionary note, however, the Goat does need to keep a watchful eye over his level of expenditure. Without a certain restraint he could find he is spending more than he anticipated and this could mean that he will have to budget carefully in the early part of 1996. The Goat also needs to deal with important forms and items of correspondence with care. A delayed reply or an oversight could cause problems and take a lot of time to sort out.

Generally, however, the Pig year will have been a pleasing year for the Goat. By pursuing his objectives and following up any opportunities that he sees, he will have made good progress and have accomplished much of which he can be proud.

The Year of the Rat starts on 19 February and is going to be another pleasing year for him. The Goat can make progress in many of his activities over the year as well as look forward to having some enjoyable times with those around him.

To make the most of the year, however, the Goat needs to decide upon his objectives and priorities. If not, he could squander his energies by getting involved in too many activities all at the same time or just going from one activity to another without achieving as much as he could. By giving himself some goal or specific task to go after, the

THE GOAT

Goat will be able to use his time constructively and achieve more as a result. So, if there is something that he wishes to achieve, no matter what area of his life it might concern, he should pursue his aims wholeheartedly. In 1996 he will find that bold and determined action on his part will bring positive results. The Rat year can be a constructive year for him but the initiative and the effort must come from the Goat.

In his work the Goat can make particularly good progress. Throughout the year there will be several opportunities that he can pursue and many Goats will take on new and more interesting responsibilities as the year progresses. The Goat should be forthcoming about any new ideas he has and if he has been thinking about launching a new project, this would be a good year to start. He will also be helped throughout the year by the co-operative attitude of those around him and would do well to listen carefully to any advice he is given by those with experience greater than his own. There will be much wisdom in their words.

Those Goats seeking work should also remain determined and follow up any openings that they see. Many will make good headway in their quest for work, often at a time when they least expect it. If they are able to add to their skills during the year, they could find that this will do much to enhance their prospects, but the main thing in 1996 is to keep trying! The spring and autumn months could prove a particularly positive time for all those looking for work or wanting to advance their career.

The Goat can also look forward to an improvement in his financial situation during the year and some Goats could receive money from an unexpected source. However, despite the financial good fortune that the Goat will enjoy, he should not become complacent in his financial dealings. Sometimes the Goat can be indulgent and spend his money rather too freely and in 1996 he should try not to squander any spare cash he may have. If he is able to set some aside for a specific purpose or invest in a savings scheme he could find this will be useful for him at a later date. The Goat will also enjoy several strokes of luck over the year and could do well to enter any competition that catches his eye.

Domestically, this will be a pleasing year for the Goat and he can look forward to some memorable and happy family occasions. Those around him will be most supportive and the Goat should make every effort to involve his family in his activities as well as be open in discussing his ideas and plans. He will also find joint projects around his home, particularly of a DIY nature, will prove most satisfying and he will be pleased with some of the home improvements that he and his family are able to carry out. The Goat's social life will also bring him much pleasure and many Goats will establish some new and worthwhile friendships as the year progresses. It is also another highly favourable year for romance and the unattached Goat or those Goats seeking new friends would do well to make every effort to go out more and get in contact with others. Matters of the heart are especially well aspected and for the unattached, a chance meeting in the early months of the year could prove most significant.

Most Goats will generally enjoy good health over the year, but any who do not get much exercise during the day will find that some additional physical activity – even if it is just a brisk walk – will do much to improve their sense of well-being. Also, as this will be quite a busy year, it is important that the Goat does set a regular time aside for his own hobbies and interests. With his artistic skills, he could find creative activities particularly enjoyable and relaxing. He should also ensure that he gets away for at least one holiday over the year. He will find that the travelling he undertakes will go well and any breaks he has will prove beneficial for him.

Generally, 1996 will be a constructive year for the Goat and with a determined attitude he can achieve much. He needs to decide upon his priorities, plan his activities and then act. Good fortune favours much of what he does and it rests with him to take advantage of the trends that prevail. Providing he is careful in money matters and arranges his activities well, he will find this a pleasing, constructive and satisfying year.

As far as the different types of Goat are concerned, this will be a most satisfying year for the *Metal Goat*. He can look forward to some pleasing times with his family and friends and his social life will be far more active than it has been in recent years. For any Metal Goat who may have felt lonely or in need of friendship, this is an ideal year to go out more and perhaps get in contact with a local club or society. Over the year there will be some excellent opportunities for him to make new friends and add to his acquaintances. The Metal Goat will also obtain much satisfaction from a new interest that he takes up and if he is a collector, particularly of art and/or antiques, he could be fortunate in some purchases he makes. Indeed, by using his time wisely and constructively, 1996 will prove a most enjoyable and fulfilling year for him. The Metal Goat will also have good fortune in financial matters, although it would still be in his interests to keep a watch over his general level of spending and not take undue risks with his finances. He will, however, enjoy any travelling and holidays he takes over the year and outdoor activities are likely to give him particular pleasure. For those Metal Goats who enjoy gardening, walking, following sport or spending time in the countryside, the year will contain many satisfying moments. Generally this will be a pleasurable year for the Metal Goat, although if he does have any concerns he should not hesitate to seek the opinions of others. His family will be most supportive over the year and be willing to help him with his various activities. This is a year which holds much promise for him and it rests with him to make the most of the favourable trends that prevail.

This is a year of considerable potential for the *Water Goat*. Several changes will take place and while, at the time, these may cause him some anxiety, the long-term result could be very much in his interests. Throughout the year the Water Goat will need to be flexible and adaptable in his outlook and take advantage of any opportunities that present themselves. Often, after unexpected developments, new opportunities do arise and it is these that the Water Goat should pursue. Sometimes he can be resistant to change, but in 1996 he does need to overcome his reticence and in all his activities he should aim to be bold, determined and positive. This year he can go a long way towards realizing his potential and securing his ambitions, but it rests with him to act and give of his best. In their work many Water Goats will take on new and often exciting responsibilities and there will be several excellent opportunities to improve upon their present position. Throughout the Rat year, those around the Water Goat will be most supportive and if he has any doubts or uncertainties about any decisions he has to take, he should not hesitate to seek their advice. He does, however, need to exercise care in his spending and while financial matters will generally go well, this is not a year in which he can afford to be too indulgent. The Water Goat's family and social life will give him much pleasure and many Water Goats can look forward to some exciting news, either concerning a member of the family or a close friend. For those Water Goats who may have experienced some personal sadness in recent years, this year will generally mark an upturn in their fortunes and those who may have been feeling lonely would do well to make every effort to go out more and perhaps join a local club. They will be glad they did. Generally, 1996 can be a year of opportunity and progress for the Water Goat and it rests with him to decide what he wants to do and to go after his objectives. He must, however, be flexible in the face of change and be prepared to act positively. Much is possible, but the amount he achieves is dependent on his efforts and attitude. For the enterprising Water Goat, this is a year of many possibilities and, for much of the year, luck is on his side.

This will be an important and significant year for the *Wood Goat*. During the year he will need to evaluate his present position and think about his future objectives. Changes are afoot and opportunities, particularly later in the year, will abound. To take advantage of the trends that prevail, the Wood Goat will need to have some idea of what he wishes to do and attain. If he wishes to move, to seek another job or go after a personal ambition, this is possible, but he does need to have a clear idea of his objectives. If not, 1996, with all its splendid opportunities, could quickly drift by, leaving the Wood Goat with little to show for his efforts. The message for Wood Goats in 1996 is to reflect, plan and follow any opportunities that they see. In addition to making good progress in his work, the Wood Goat should try to add to his skills and go on any courses that he feels might be useful. Anything that he can do to widen his experience and extend his skills will do much to enhance his longer-term prospects. Throughout the year the Wood Goat will enjoy much support and encouragement from his family and friends, and at all times he should remain mindful of their views and advice. They do speak with his best interests at heart and some advice a more senior relative or colleague gives him early in 1996 could prove invaluable to him over the next few years. The Wood Goat will be fortunate in financial matters in 1996 and many Wood Goats could receive an additional and unexpected sum of money over the year. However, despite the financial good fortune most of them will enjoy, the Wood Goat still needs to exercise restraint in his spending – several large purchases that he makes could deplete his savings and, without care, he could find these difficult to replenish. As this will be a relatively active year for him, the Wood Goat may not have as much time for his own interests as he may like. However, he should still make sure that he sets a regular time aside for recreational pursuits and that he allows himself time to adequately rest, relax and unwind. If not, he could find himself tired and below par and not making as much of the year as he otherwise could.

This will be a busy and eventful year for the *Fire Goat*. There will be many demands on his time and sometimes he may despair about all that is being asked of him. However, if he organizes his activities well and decides on his priorities, he will be surprised and delighted by just how much he is able to accomplish. The main thing for the Fire Goat in 1996 is not to over-commit himself or try to do too many things all at the same time. He can achieve a great deal over the year but it needs planning, organization and a sense of priorities. In his work, the Fire Goat can make substantial progress and any Fire Goat seeking work or wanting a change of employment should particularly keep alert for opportunities in the springtime – April and May could both be important months for career matters. Many Fire Goats will take on new and more challenging responsibilities as the year develops and most will see an improvement in their financial situation. However, as with all Goats in 1996, the Fire Goat does need to keep a close watch over his spending and if he does have any spare money, he would do well to set some aside for a particular purpose rather than spend it too readily. The Fire Goat will lead an enjoyable social life over the year and can look forward to attending some memorable and sometimes unusual social functions. His family life will also give him much satisfaction and he will take great pride in the successes enjoyed by a younger relation. However, in view of the busy nature of the year, if ever he feels too much is being asked of him, he should not hesitate to ask for assistance or seek advice. Those around him will be only too willing to help and the Fire Goat is fortunate in that he has so many he can turn to for advice and assistance should he need it. Although 1996 will be a demanding year for him, it will still be a year which contains much happiness and he will be able to make some positive strides in his career.

This will be both an important and enjoyable year for the *Earth Goat*. He can look forward to making substantial progress in many of his activities as well as having some splendid times with his family and friends. Socially, 1996 will be a good year for him and many Earth Goats will make some new and important friendships over the course of the year. The aspects for romance are particularly strong. However, while the year will contain much happiness for the Earth Goat, he should try not to let his social life encroach too much on his everyday duties. If he is in education this could prove an important year for him and he would be wise not to neglect his studies or get distracted by other matters. In 1996 he does need to get his priorities right! Generally, academic matters will go favourably for him and by extending his skills and qualifications he will do much to enhance his future prospects. Travel could also figure prominently over the year and those Earth Goats who wish to improve on their language skills or who have time at their disposal could benefit from any time they spend visiting another country. Throughout the year the Earth Goat will be well-supported by his family and he would do well to remain mindful of their views and feelings. While there may sometimes be areas of disagreement – particularly with some of his older relatives – the Earth Goat should remember that they do have his best interests at heart. The Earth Goat will also need to exercise care in his spending over the year and, as far as possible, avoid stretching his resources too far. Generally, however, 1996 will be a positive and fulfilling year for him, with some excellent opportunities to pursue towards the end of it. The later part of the year, from September onwards, could prove a most successful and meaningful time for him.

# FAMOUS GOATS

Isaac Asimov, W. H. Auden, Jane Austen, Anne Bancroft, Boris Becker, Cilla Black, Ian Botham, Elkie Brooks, George Burns, Leslie Caron, John le Carré, Coco Chanel, Nat 'King' Cole, Harry Connick Jr, Catherine Deneuve, John Denver, Charles Dickens, Ken Dodd, Sir Arthur Conan Doyle, Umberto Eco, Douglas Fairbanks, Keith Floyd, Dame Margot Fonteyn, Anna Ford, Paul Gascoigne, Mel Gibson, Newt Gingrich, Paul Michael Glaser, Sharon Gless, Mikhail Gorbachev, Larry Hagman, George Harrison, Sir Edmund Hillary, Hulk Hogan, Isabelle Huppert, Julio Iglesias, Mick Jagger, Paul Keating, Ben Kingsley, David Kossoff, Doris Lessing, Peter Lilley, Franz Liszt, John Major, Michelangelo, Cliff Michelmore, Joni Mitchell, Frank Muir, Iris Murdoch, Rupert Murdoch, Mussolini, Leonard Nimoy, Robert de Niro, Oliver North, Des O'Connor, Sinead O'Connor, Lord Olivier, Michael Palin, Alain Prost, Keith Richards, Sir Malcolm Sargent, William Shatner, Mike Smith, Freddie Starr, Lord Tebbit, Leslie Thomas, Lana Turner, Desmond Tutu, Mark Twain, Rudolph Valentino, Vangelis, Terry Venables, Lech Walesa, Barbara Walters, John Wayne, Tuesday Weld, Fay Weldon, Bruce Willis, Debra Winger, Paul Young.

2 FEBRUARY 1908 ～ 21 JANUARY 1909     *Earth Monkey*

20 FEBRUARY 1920 ～ 7 FEBRUARY 1921     *Metal Monkey*

6 FEBRUARY 1932 ～ 25 JANUARY 1933     *Water Monkey*

25 JANUARY 1944 ～ 12 FEBRUARY 1945     *Wood Monkey*

12 FEBRUARY 1956 ～ 30 JANUARY 1957     *Fire Monkey*

30 JANUARY 1968 ～ 16 FEBRUARY 1969     *Earth Monkey*

16 FEBRUARY 1980 ～ 4 FEBRUARY 1981     *Metal Monkey*

4 FEBRUARY 1992 ～ 22 JANUARY 1993     *Water Monkey*

# THE
# MONKEY

# THE PERSONALITY OF THE MONKEY

Man needs, for his happiness, not only the enjoyment of
this or that, but hope and enterprise and change.
                                    – *Bertrand Russell: a Monkey*

The Monkey is born under the sign of fantasy. He is imaginative, inquisitive and loves to keep an eye on everything that is going on around him. He is never backward in offering advice or trying to sort out the problems of others. He likes to be helpful and his advice is invariably sensible and reliable.

The Monkey is intelligent, well-read and always eager to learn. He has an extremely good memory and there are many Monkeys who have made particularly good linguists. The Monkey is also a convincing talker and enjoys taking part in discussions and debates. His friendly, self-assured manner can be very persuasive and he usually has little trouble in winning people round to his way of thinking – it is for this reason that the Monkey often excels in politics and public speaking. He is also particularly adept in PR work, teaching and any job which involves selling.

The Monkey can, however, be crafty, cunning and occasionally dishonest, and he will seize on any opportunity to make a quick gain or outsmart his opponents. He has so much charm and guile that people often don't realize what he is up to until it is too late. But despite his resourceful nature, the Monkey does run the risk of outsmarting even himself. He has so much confidence in his abilities that he rarely listens to advice or is prepared to accept help from anyone. He likes to help others but prefers to rely on his own judgement when dealing with his own affairs.

Another characteristic of the Monkey is that he is extremely good at solving problems and has a happy knack of extricating himself (and others) from the most hopeless of positions. He is the master of self-preservation.

With so many diverse talents the Monkey is able to make considerable sums of money, but he does like to enjoy life and will think nothing of spending his money on some exotic holiday or luxury which he has had his eye on. He can, however, become very envious if someone else has got what he wants.

The Monkey is an original thinker and, despite his love of company, he cherishes his independence. He has to have the freedom to act as he wants and any Monkey who feels hemmed in or bound by too many restrictions can soon become unhappy. Likewise, if anything becomes too boring or monotonous, he soon loses interest and turns his attention to something else. The Monkey lacks persistence and this can often hamper his progress. He is also easily distracted, a tendency which all Monkeys should try to overcome. The Monkey should concentrate on one thing at a time and by doing so will almost certainly achieve more in the long run.

The Monkey is a good organizer and, even though he may behave slightly erratically at times, he will invariably have some plan at the back of his mind. On the odd occasion when his plans do not quite work out, he is usually quite happy to shrug his shoulders and put it down to experience. He will rarely make the same mistake twice and throughout his life he will try his hand at many things.

The Monkey likes to impress and is rarely without followers or admirers. There are many who are attracted to him by his good looks, his sense of humour or simply because he instils so much confidence.

Monkeys usually marry young and for it to be a success their partner must allow them time to pursue their many interests and the opportunity to indulge in their love of travel. The Monkey has to have variety in his life and is especially well-suited to those born under the sociable and outgoing signs of the Rat, Dragon, Pig and Goat. The Ox, Rabbit, Snake and Dog will also be enchanted by the Monkey's resourceful and outgoing nature, but he is likely to exasperate the Rooster and Horse, and the Tiger will have little patience for his tricks. A relationship between two Monkeys will work well – they will understand each other and be able to assist each other in their various enterprises.

The female Monkey is intelligent, extremely observant and a shrewd judge of character. Her opinions and views are often highly valued, and, having such a persuasive nature, she invariably gets her own way. She has many interests and involves herself in a wide variety of activities. She pays great attention to her appearance, is an elegant dresser and likes to take particular care over her hair. She can also be a most caring and doting parent and will have many good and loyal friends.

Provided the Monkey can curb his desire to take part in all that is going on around him and concentrate on one thing at a time, he can usually achieve what he wants in life. Should he suffer any disappointments, he is bound to bounce back. The Monkey is a survivor and his life is usually both colourful and very eventful.

# THE FIVE DIFFERENT TYPES OF MONKEY

In addition to the 12 signs of the Chinese zodiac, there are five elements and these have a strengthening or moderating influence on the sign. The effects of the five elements on the Monkey are described below, together with the years in which the elements were exercising their influence. Therefore all Monkeys born in 1920 and 1980 are Metal Monkeys, those born in 1932 and 1992 are Water Monkeys, and so on.

## Metal Monkey: 1920, 1980
The Metal Monkey is very strong-willed. He sets about everything he does with a dogged determination and often prefers to work independently rather than with others. He is ambitious, wise and confident, and is certainly not afraid of hard work. He is very astute in financial matters and usually chooses his investments well. Despite his somewhat independent nature, the Metal Monkey enjoys attending parties and social occasions and is particularly warm and caring towards his loved ones.

## Water Monkey: 1932, 1992
The Water Monkey is versatile, determined and perceptive. He also has more discipline than some of the other Monkeys and is prepared to work towards a certain goal rather than be distracted by something else. He is not

always open about his true intentions and when questioned can be particularly evasive. He can be sensitive to criticism but also very persuasive and usually has little trouble in getting others to fall in with his plans. He has a very good understanding of human nature and relates well to others.

## Wood Monkey: 1944

This Monkey is efficient, methodical and extremely conscientious. He is also highly imaginative and is always trying to capitalize on new ideas or learning new skills. Occasionally his enthusiasm can get the better of him and he can get very agitated when things do not quite work out as he had hoped. He does, however, have a very adventurous streak in him and is not afraid of taking risks. He also loves travel. He is usually held in great esteem by his friends and colleagues.

## Fire Monkey: 1896, 1956

The Fire Monkey is intelligent, full of vitality and has no trouble in commanding the respect of others. He is imaginative and has wide interests, although sometimes these can distract him from more useful and profitable work. He is very competitive and always likes to be involved in everything that is going on. He can be stubborn if he does not get his own way and he sometimes tries to indoctrinate those who are less strong-willed than himself. The Fire Monkey is a lively character, popular with the opposite sex and extremely loyal to his partner.

## Earth Monkey: 1908, 1968

The Earth Monkey tends to be studious and well-read, and can become quite distinguished in his chosen line of work. He is less outgoing than some of the other types of Monkey and prefers quieter and more solid pursuits. He has high principles, a very caring nature and can be most generous to those less fortunate than himself. He is usually successful in handling financial matters and can become very wealthy in old age. He has a calming influence on those around him and is respected and well liked by those he meets. He is, however, especially careful about whom he lets into his confidence.

# PROSPECTS FOR THE MONKEY IN 1996

The Chinese New Year starts on 19 February 1996. Until then, the old year, the Year of the Pig, is still making its presence felt.

The Year of the Pig (31 January 1995 to 18 February 1996) will have been a reasonable year for the Monkey. Admittedly, not all his plans and hopes for the year may have materialized, but the Monkey will still have achieved much. In what remains of the Pig year he would do well to remain alert for opportunities so he can use his skills. In October and November 1995 there could be some excellent opportunities for him to pursue in his work and he should actively follow up any openings that he sees. It would also be in his interests to complete any outstanding matters at this time. The Rat year promises to be an excellent and exciting year for him and as far as possible the Monkey should try to free himself of any unfinished business in preparation for it. This particularly applies to dealing with unanswered correspondence and resolving any trouble-some bureaucratic matters that he might have. With a concerted effort, the Monkey will be well pleased with what he is able to accomplish at this time.

The one thing that the Monkey should avoid is to over-commit himself or take on too many activities at the same time. Throughout the Pig year he will find he will achieve better results by concentrating on specific matters rather than attempting too much. He should also avoid taking unnecessary risks – although he has a resourceful nature, throughout the Pig year he should avoid pushing his Monkey luck too far! The Monkey can also look forward to an enjoyable domestic and social life in the closing stages of the year. His social life in particular will be busy and he will find himself much in demand with his family and friends. Those Monkeys who are unattached will also have several opportunities to make new friends, particularly in the weeks leading up to Christmas.

The closing months of the Pig year can be a constructive, favourable and enjoyable time for the Monkey. However, if he has any opportunity to think now about what he would like to achieve in the next 12 months, he will find he will be better able to take advantage of the improved trends that await him.

The Year of the Rat starts on 19 February and is going to be one of the best years that the Monkey has enjoyed for some time. In almost every area of his life he will do well and opportunities for progress abound. The Monkey is blessed with a most resourceful nature and this will be a year in which he will not only enjoy himself but be able to make the most of his considerable abilities.

Throughout the year those around the Monkey will be most supportive and will do much to help him with his various activities. And although the Monkey tends to rely a lot on his own efforts, it would be in his interests to let others share in his plans and remain mindful of their views. Indeed, he will find progress much easier if he avails himself of a helping hand rather than relying solely on his own efforts.

The Monkey's family life in particular will be most satisfying and many Monkeys can look forward to some memorable family occasions over the year. This can include an addition to the family or success enjoyed by a close relation. For the unattached Monkey, the aspects for romance, engagement and marriage are excellent. Monkeys traditionally get on well with those born in a Rat year and those Monkeys who are romantically linked to a Rat will find this an especially happy year.

In addition to a pleasurable home and family life, the Monkey will also have an active social life. There will be a variety of functions to attend and many Monkeys will have plenty of opportunities to widen their circle of acquaintances as the year progresses. With his charm and personable manner the Monkey will impress many and some of those he meets could prove helpful to him in the future. For those Monkeys who may have felt lonely in recent years or are seeking friends, 1996 will be a much happier year. These Monkeys would do well to go out

YOUR CHINESE HOROSCOPE 1996

more and perhaps consider joining a local club or society. Positive action on their part will bring pleasing results.

The Monkey will also derive considerable pleasure from his hobbies and interests over the year. However, while this will be a favourable year for him, he would do well to overcome his rather restless tendencies. With so much happening in 1996 there could be a temptation for him to jump from activity to activity rather than concentrate on one thing at a time. If the Monkey could impose a little more discipline over his activities rather than involving himself in too much, he would find his efforts bringing him considerably more satisfaction.

Travel is well aspected over the year and those Monkeys who enjoy outdoor activities can look forward to some particularly pleasing times.

The Monkey will also do well in his work. Many Monkeys will be given new and more interesting responsibilities over the year and the opportunities for promotion or a move to a better position are excellent. Also, if the Monkey wishes to change the nature of his work, he should make enquiries or contact those who may be able to help him. By acting positively and taking action, he will be successful in achieving many of his aims. Monkeys seeking work should particularly remain alert for opportunities to pursue. The Monkey is blessed with a most resourceful and adaptable nature and he could meet with success in a type of work which he may not have considered before. The Year of the Rat is very much a year of opportunity for the Monkey and all Monkeys would do well to promote their talents as well as make the most of their enterprising natures. For the determined Monkey, this can be a truly rewarding year.

The Monkey will enjoy good fortune in financial matters and most Monkeys will end the year in a much healthier financial state than at the beginning. Some shrewd investments could prove successful and if the Monkey is able to set some spare funds aside for a long-term savings scheme, he could find these will build into a worthwhile asset in years to come. However, despite his financial good fortune, the Monkey ought not trust his luck too far and should remain wary of speculative or dubious ventures.

Generally, 1996 will be an excellent year for the Monkey and it rests with him to make the most of the progressive trends that prevail. Domestically and socially, he can look forward to some happy times and in his work and career there will be some good opportunities to improve upon his position. Money matters will also go well. In 1996 much is in the Monkey's favour, but to make the most of these auspicious trends, he needs to decide upon his priorities and concentrate his efforts on specific matters rather than spread his energies too widely. With determination and his usual positive attitude, his accomplishments over the year can be considerable.

As far as the different types of Monkey are concerned, this will be a year of considerable opportunity for the *Metal Monkey*. He can make significant progress in most areas of his life as well as enjoying much of the year. His family and social life in particular will give him much pleasure and those around him will be supportive and encouraging. However, he would do well to remain mindful of their advice and views and, even if he may not agree with all he is told, should remember that they often speak with the benefit of experience. The Metal Monkey may sometimes feel he is able to achieve what he wants by relying solely on his own efforts, but this is not always the case! To get the best from this auspicious year, he does need to act in unison with others. His social life will be active and enjoyable and many Metal Monkeys can look forward to building some important and meaningful friendships as the year progresses. The summer months in particular are likely to be a happy and enjoyable time. The Metal Monkey will generally have good fortune in money matters, but he should still be wary about getting involved in risky or speculative schemes. If in doubt over any financial matter he would do well to seek advice rather than take risks. The Metal Monkey will also derive considerable pleasure from his hobbies and interests over the year and if he is able to further his interests and skills in any way he should do so. Anything constructive he can do will be very much to his future advantage. Many Metal Monkeys could find that a self-taught skill or talent they have could lead to some unexpected opportunities. Those involved in education will make good progress and while the Metal Monkey may feel there are other matters which he may prefer to do, the time he devotes to his studies will be well rewarded. He will also very much enjoy the travelling that he undertakes over the year, particularly to destinations he has not visited before. Generally, 1996 will be a splendid and happy year for him and it rests with him to use his time wisely and to pursue the opportunities that the year will bring. For the determined and enterprising Metal Monkey, this can be a momentous year.

This will be a pleasant and enjoyable year for the *Water Monkey*. If, in recent times, he has felt weighed down by problems or not had as much time for family activities and his interests as he would have liked, this will now change. This year will mark a distinct upturn in his fortunes and he will have more time to do what he wants. Given his resourceful nature, he is certain to use his time well. If there have been any hobbies or interests that have been intriguing him, this is an ideal year to find out more. He could find creative activities such as photography, art, writing or music especially enjoyable and relaxing. Or, if he wants to carry out some improvements to his home and garden, he will now have more time to carry these out. The Water Monkey can achieve much over the year and by deciding upon his activities he will be delighted with what he is able to accomplish. He can also look forward to some pleasing financial news over the year and some Water Monkeys could receive an additional sum of money from an unexpected source. Any Water Monkey who moves over the year will be satisfied with how it works out and a change in area could lead to new friends, an improved social life and new opportunities. The Water Monkey can also look forward to some memorable times with his family. Many Water Monkeys will have good reason for a family celebration over the year – this could include the marriage of a close relation or birth of a grandchild. Generally, 1996 will be a most auspicious year for the Water Monkey and it rests with him to decide want he wants to achieve over the year and then go after his objectives. With a positive attitude, he can accomplish much and, for most of the year, luck is on his side.

This will be a year of considerable opportunity for the *Wood Monkey*. Throughout he will be able to make better use of his skills and talents and make pleasing progress in many of his activities. In particular, work matters are most favourably aspected. Many Wood Monkeys will be given new and more stimulating responsibilities and the aspects are also encouraging for those Wood Monkeys seeking work or wanting to change their position. The early part of the year could prove a significant time, with March to May being important months. Throughout the year the Wood Monkey would do well to remain alert for opportunities to pursue and not be afraid of acting on his initiative. The rewards for the bold and enterprising Wood Monkey can be great indeed. The Wood Monkey will also enjoy some pleasing financial news over the year and most Wood Monkeys will see a significant improvement in their financial situation. An investment made or a savings policy taken out now could prove successful over the longer-term. However, in all his financial undertakings, the Wood Monkey would do well not to take undue risks or commit himself to any large transaction without checking the details beforehand. Although this is a favourable year for financial matters, he cannot afford to be complacent or careless when dealing with his finances. Those Wood Monkeys who enjoy antiques or are collectors could make some worthwhile purchases in 1996 and all Wood Monkeys would do well to keep alert for interesting buys over the year. The Wood Monkey's domestic and social life will give him much pleasure and those around him will provide much useful support for his various activities. If, however, he has any large projects that he wishes to carry out around his home, he should try to involve those around him in the project rather than carry out the work single-handed. He will find joint projects will prove satisfying for all concerned as well as being quicker and easier to accomplish! The Wood Monkey will enjoy the travel that he undertakes over the year and any holidays or short breaks are likely to go well and be beneficial for him. If he does not get much exercise during the day, he could find that some additional walking or an activity such as swimming or cycling will do much to improve his level of fitness. This will be a pleasing and satisfying year for him and by pursuing the opportunities that he sees and making the best use of his many talents he will very much enjoy the year.

This will be both an auspicious and enjoyable year for the *Fire Monkey*. He will be able to make pleasing progress in many of his activities and in his work he could realize some of his ambitions. He should follow up any openings he sees and promote himself, his skills and talents as much as he can. In 1996 he can make significant strides in his career and it rests with him to act in a positive manner and make the most of his many abilities. Any Fire Monkey seeking work or feeling dissatisfied with his present position should again follow up any vacancies that interest him. Throughout the year the Fire Monkey can achieve much, but his results are heavily dependent upon his attitude and level of determination. April to June could prove an important time for career matters. The Fire Monkey will also enjoy an improvement in his financial situation over the year and an investment or savings policy that he takes out could turn into a useful asset in years to come.

He will also do well with some purchases he makes and by remaining alert he could acquire some items for himself and his home at most advantageous prices. Domestically, this will also be a pleasing year and the Fire Monkey will delight in the progress and successes enjoyed by those close to him. Any encouragement and guidance he feels he can give will be much appreciated, although if there happens to be any family matter causing him concern, he would do well to let his views be known rather than keeping them to himself. The Fire Monkey will also lead a satisfying social life over the year. Any Fire Monkey who may have experienced some recent sadness or feels in need of more friends will be pleased to find his social life will pick up quite considerably. Travel is also well aspected and a family holiday that the Fire Monkey takes could turn out to be one of the best he has had for many years. Generally, in most areas of his life, he can do well. However his level of achievements are partly dependent on how much he asserts himself. He has the skills, the talents and the personality to do well. The aspects are favourable and it rests with him to make the most of the auspicious trends that prevail.

This will be an eventful year for the *Earth Monkey*. In many areas of his life he will see changes taking place and while some of these may cause times of uncertainty, the events of the year will work out in his favour. Out of change will come new and brighter opportunities and the resourceful Earth Monkey is often at his best when facing new challenges and opportunities. In his work, much progress is possible. Most Earth Monkeys will change the nature of their duties over the year and many will move to more responsible and rewarding positions. Throughout the year, particularly from April to June, the Earth Monkey should keep alert for opportunities and vacancies to pursue and ways he can put his skills to better use. By acting boldly and positively, he can accomplish a great deal. Those Earth Monkeys seeking work should also follow up any opportunities they see as well as considering types of work new to them. Earth Monkeys are blessed with much versatility and they could find a different area of work will reveal talents and skills they did not know they possessed! The Earth Monkey's family life will be busy and most enjoyable. Those around him will be supportive and give him much useful encouragement and advice over the year. He will also take great delight in the progress enjoyed by a younger relation and his home life will give him much satisfaction. For the unattached Earth Monkey, this could prove a memorable year and many will meet their future partner, get engaged or married. The Earth Monkey will generally fare well in financial matters over the year, although he could face some expenses connected with his accommodation. If this occurs, he does need to make sure that he budgets accordingly and is fully aware of any obligations he may be placed under. There will also be several opportunities for the Earth Monkey to travel in 1996 – sometimes considerable distances – and he will find the journeys he undertakes will go well. Generally, 1996 holds much promise for the Earth Monkey and he will see positive progress in most areas of his life. He has many talents and during the year he should make every effort to make the most of himself and the opportunities that arise. For the go-ahead Earth Monkey, this can be a successful and memorable year.

# FAMOUS MONKEYS

Francesca Annis, Michael Aspel, Mike Atherton, J. M. Barrie, David Bellamy, Jacqueline Bisset, Bjorn Borg, Victor Borge, Dave Brubeck, Yul Brynner, Julius Caesar, Marti Caine, Princess Caroline of Monaco, Johnny Cash, Jacques Chirac, Chelsea Clinton, Joe Cocker, Colette, John Constable, Alistair Cooke, David Copperfield, Joan Crawford, Timothy Dalton, Bette Davis, Bo Derek, Danny De Vito, Jonathan Dimbleby, Jason Donovan, Michael Douglas, Mia Farrow, Michael Fish, Carrie Fisher, F. Scott Fitzgerald, Ian Fleming, Dick Francis, Fiona Fullerton, Paul Gauguin, Jerry Hall, Tom Hanks, Roy Hattersley, Stephen Hendry, Patricia Highsmith, Harry Houdini, Tony Jacklin, P. D. James, Pope John Paul II, Lyndon B. Johnson, Edward Kennedy, Nigel Kennedy, Jonathan King, Gladys Knight, Lord Lawson, Leo McKern, Walter Matthau, Princess Michael of Kent, Kylie Minogue, Martina Navratilova, Jack Nicklaus, Derek Nimmo, Peter O'Toole, Charlie Parker, Chris Patten, Anthony Perkins, Robert Powell, Mario Puzo, Debbie Reynolds, Tim Rice, Little Richard, Angela Rippon, Mary Robinson, Diana Ross, Boz Scaggs, Michael Schumacher, Paul Scofield, Tom Selleck, Omar Sharif, Wilbur Smith, Koo Stark, Rod Stewart, Michael Stich, Jacques Tati, Elizabeth Taylor, Dame Kiri Te Kanawa, Harry Truman, Leonardo da Vinci, the Duchess of Windsor, Bobby Womack.

| | |
|---|---|
| 22 JANUARY 1909 ～ 9 FEBRUARY 1910 | *Earth Rooster* |
| 8 FEBRUARY 1921 ～ 27 JANUARY 1922 | *Metal Rooster* |
| 26 JANUARY 1933 ～ 13 FEBRUARY 1934 | *Water Rooster* |
| 13 FEBRUARY 1945 ～ 1 FEBRUARY 1946 | *Wood Rooster* |
| 31 JANUARY 1957 ～ 17 FEBRUARY 1958 | *Fire Rooster* |
| 17 FEBRUARY 1969 ～ 5 FEBRUARY 1970 | *Earth Rooster* |
| 5 FEBRUARY 1981 ～ 24 JANUARY 1982 | *Metal Rooster* |
| 23 JANUARY 1993 ～ 9 FEBRUARY 1994 | *Water Rooster* |

# THE
# ROOSTER

# THE PERSONALITY OF THE ROOSTER

> Life is not a problem to be solved but a reality to be experienced.
>
> — *Søren Kierkegaard: a Rooster*

The Rooster is born under the sign of candour. He has a flamboyant and colourful personality and is meticulous in all that he does. He is an excellent organizer and wherever possible likes to plan his various activities well in advance.

The Rooster is highly intelligent and usually very well read. He has a good sense of humour and is an effective and persuasive speaker. He loves discussion and enjoys taking part in any sort of debate. He has no hesitation in speaking his mind and is forthright in his views. He does, however, lack tact and can easily damage his reputation or cause offence by some thoughtless remark or action. The Rooster also has a very volatile nature and he should always try to avoid acting on the spur of the moment.

The Rooster is usually very dignified in his manner and conducts himself with an air of confidence and authority. He is adept at handling financial matters and, as with most things, he organizes his financial affairs with considerable skill. He chooses his investments well and is capable of achieving great wealth. Most Roosters save or use their money wisely, but there are a few who are the reverse and are notorious spendthrifts. Fortunately, the Rooster has great earning capacity and is rarely without sufficient funds to tide himself over.

Another characteristic of the Rooster is that he invariably carries a notebook or scraps of paper around with him. He is constantly writing himself reminders or noting down important facts lest he forgets – the Rooster cannot abide inefficiency and conducts all his activities in an orderly, precise and methodical manner.

The Rooster is usually very ambitious, but can be unrealistic in some of the things that he hopes to achieve. He occasionally lets his imagination run away with him and, while he does not like any interference in the things that he does, it would be in his own interests if he were to listen to the views of others a little more often. He also does not like criticism and if he feels anybody is doubting his judgement or prying too closely into his affairs, he is certain to let his feelings be known. He can also be rather self-centred and stubborn over relatively trivial matters, but to compensate for this he is reliable, honest and trustworthy, and this is very much appreciated by all who come into contact with him.

Roosters born between the hours of five and seven (both at dawn and sundown) tend to be the most extrovert of their sign, but all Roosters like to lead an active social life and enjoy attending parties and big functions. The Rooster usually has a wide circle of friends and is able to build up influential contacts with remarkable ease. He often belongs to several clubs and societies and involves himself in a variety of different activities. He is particularly interested in the environment, humanitarian affairs and anything affecting the welfare of others. The Rooster has a very caring nature and will do much to help those less fortunate than himself.

He also gets much pleasure from gardening and, while

he may not always spend as much time in the garden as he would like, his garden is invariably well-kept and extremely productive.

The Rooster is generally very distinguished in his appearance and, if his job permits, he will wear an official uniform with great pride and dignity. He is not averse to publicity and takes great delight in being the centre of attention. He often does well at PR work or any job which brings him into contact with the media. He also makes a very good teacher.

The female Rooster leads a varied and interesting life. She involves herself in many different activities and there are some who wonder how she can achieve so much. She often holds very strong views and, like her male counterpart, has no hesitation in speaking her mind or telling others how she thinks things should be done. She is supremely efficient and well-organized and her home is usually very neat and tidy. She has good taste in clothes and usually wears smart but very practical outfits.

The Rooster usually has a large family and as a parent takes a particularly active interest in the education of his children. He is very loyal to his partner and will find that he is especially well-suited to those born under the signs of the Snake, Horse, Ox and Dragon. Provided they do not interfere too much in the Rooster's various activities, the Rat, Tiger, Goat and Pig can also establish a good relationship with him, but two Roosters together are likely to squabble and irritate each other. The rather sensitive Rabbit will find the Rooster a bit too blunt for his liking, and the Rooster will quickly become exasperated by the ever-inquisitive and artful Monkey. He will also find it difficult to get on with the Dog.

If the Rooster can overcome his volatile nature and exercise more tact in some of the things that he says, he will go far in life. He is capable and talented and will invariably make a lasting – and usually favourable – impression almost everywhere he goes.

# THE FIVE DIFFERENT TYPES OF ROOSTER

In addition to the 12 signs of the Chinese zodiac, there are five elements and these have a strengthening or moderating influence on the sign. The effects of the five elements on the Rooster are described below, together with the years in which the elements were exercising their influence. Therefore all Roosters born in 1921 and 1981 are Metal Roosters, those born in 1933 and 1993 are Water Roosters, and so on.

## Metal Rooster: 1921, 1981

The Metal Rooster is a hard and conscientious worker. He knows exactly what he wants in life and sets about everything he does in a positive and determined manner. He can at times appear abrasive and he would almost certainly do better if he were more willing to reach a compromise with others rather than hold so rigidly to his firmly held beliefs. He is very articulate and most astute when dealing with financial matters. He is loyal to his friends and often devotes much energy to working for the common good.

## Water Rooster: 1933, 1993

This Rooster has a very persuasive manner and can easily gain the co-operation of others. He is intelligent, well-read and gets much enjoyment from taking part in discussions and debates. He has a seemingly inexhaustible amount of energy and is prepared to work long hours in order to secure what he wants. He can, however, waste much valuable time worrying over minor and inconsequential details. He is approachable, has a good sense of humour and is highly regarded by others.

## Wood Rooster: 1945

The Wood Rooster is honest, reliable and often sets himself high standards. He is ambitious, but also more prepared to work in a team than some of the other types of Rooster. He usually succeeds in life but does have a tendency to get caught up in bureaucratic matters or attempt too many things all at the same time. He has wide interests, likes to travel and is very considerate and caring towards his family and friends.

## Fire Rooster: 1897, 1957

This Rooster is extremely strong-willed. He has many leadership qualities, is an excellent organizer and is most efficient in his work. Through sheer force of character he often secures his objectives, but he does have a tendency to be very forthright and not always consider the feelings of others. If the Fire Rooster can learn to be more tactful he can often succeed beyond his wildest dreams.

## Earth Rooster: 1909, 1969

This Rooster has a deep and penetrating mind. He is extremely efficient, very perceptive and is particularly astute in business and financial matters. He is also persistent and once he has set himself an objective, he will rarely allow himself to be deflected from achieving his aim. The Earth Rooster works hard and is held in great esteem by his friends and colleagues. He usually gets much enjoyment from the arts and takes a keen interest in the activities of the various members of his family.

# PROSPECTS FOR THE ROOSTER IN 1996

The Chinese New Year starts on 19 February 1996. Until then, the old year, the Year of the Pig, is still making its presence felt.

The Year of the Pig (31 January 1995 to 18 February 1996) will have been a generally favourable year for the Rooster and the remaining months of the year promise to be an interesting and fulfilling time.

The Rooster is helped in much of what he does by his efficient and orderly manner, and with a determined attitude, he can achieve much before the year ends. In his work he will continue to impress and those Roosters seeking work or wishing to transfer to a new position should remain alert for opportunities in the closing months of the Pig year. January 1996 could prove a significant month for career matters. However, the one thing all Roosters do need to watch is their candid tongue. An inopportune remark could undo much of the good achieved over the year and upset colleagues and friends unnecessarily. It is a point all Roosters would do well to remember!

The Rooster is likely to have enjoyed some financial good fortune during the Pig year and, while the closing months of the year may prove expensive, most Roosters will end the year in a much improved financial position. However, matters connected with accommodation do need careful handling and any Rooster planning to move or have work carried out on his property will need to exercise care and check all aspects of the transaction carefully. If he has doubts over any matter he would do well to seek advice.

Domestically and socially, the remaining months of the year will be an active but pleasing time. The Rooster will be much in demand with his family and friends and can look forward to attending a variety of interesting social functions. Roosters who are unattached or seeking new friends could find this a particularly active time socially.

Although the Year of the Pig will have been a generally positive year for the Rooster, it will still have been a demanding one for him. If he can set a week aside for a short break or give himself a proper rest over the Christmas and New Year holidays he will feel considerably better for doing so. Although the Rooster usually possesses much energy, he does need to renew his reserves and a break from his usually busy schedule will prove most beneficial for him.

The Year of the Rat starts on 19 February and is going to be a challenging year for the Rooster. Although he is a fine organizer, he could find that in the Rat year even the best laid plans go wrong and it may be difficult for him to make as much progress as he would like. However, while this may not be the best of years for the Rooster, it is still possible for him to get much of value from it. He will be able to widen his experience as well as lay the foundations for the considerably better times that await him in 1997.

Throughout the Rat year, however, the Rooster needs to proceed carefully. In his work he should not take undue risks and he should also pay close attention to the views and opinions of all around him. This is not a year when he can afford to go it alone or adopt too independent an attitude. To make any sort of progress in 1996 the Rooster does need the support and co-operation of others. Similarly, he would do well to keep a tight rein over his sometimes forthright nature. To speak out of turn or be too abrupt could easily impair his normally good relations with his work fellows. Provided the Rooster bears these points in mind, though, he can still make useful progress over the year. There will be chances, particularly in the springtime, for him to take on new and more varied duties and these will prove an interesting challenge for him. Also, he would do well to take advantage of any opportunity to go on courses or expand his experience. Anything constructive he can do will do much to enhance his future prospects. In some respects, the Rooster can consider 1996 as a year for taking stock of his present position, for learning and for laying the foundations for the significant advances he will be making over the next few years.

However, the Rooster does need to exercise care with financial matters in 1996. This could prove an expensive year for him and he could find that several large transactions could quickly deplete his savings. Some of these expenses will be unavoidable – particularly those connected with his accommodation – but in all financial matters it would be in the Rooster's interests to check the various prices and terms on offer. If not, he could find his outlay is greater than it need be. Similarly, he should be wary about buying items on impulse, as these could prove costly for him and he could end up regretting his purchases. Neither should he gamble nor speculate with money that he can ill afford to lose. Generally, the aspects are not good for financial matters and the Rooster does need to exercise restraint and caution in his financial dealings.

The Rooster's domestic life will, however, be generally busy over the year. In addition to the usual sterling support he gives to other members of his family, he will give particular help to a close relation who has some awkward problem to overcome. Although this may put some additional burden on the Rooster, he can be assured that his assistance will be greatly appreciated and will do much to help. When it comes to assisting others, the Rooster has many fine qualities and these are recognized and greatly appreciated.

Similarly, if the Rooster himself has any matters concerning him he should not hesitate to seek the opinions of those around him. Although he does have a tendency to keep his thoughts to himself, he will find it helpful to discuss any worries he has with others and to seek their views and opinions. He will be gratified and reassured by the support he is given.

Many Roosters will also carry out projects around their home over the year. This can include decorating or carrying out alterations and, while the work may take him longer than anticipated, the Rooster will be satisfied with the finished result. Also, any Rooster who moves over the year will find it will work out well for him and he will enjoy the opportunities and changes that a new neighbourhood will bring.

As this will be quite an active year for the Rooster, he may not have as much time for his own interests as he would like. However, no matter what demands he may face, he should make sure that he does regularly set some time aside to indulge in recreational activities and give himself the opportunity to rest and unwind. He could get particular pleasure from outdoor pursuits, and activities such as gardening, walking and exploring the countryside could prove both enjoyable and beneficial for him.

The Rooster's social life will also give him much pleasure and he can look forward to attending some enjoyable functions over the year, especially during the summer. However, throughout the year he would do well to remain mindful of the views and feelings of his friends and listen particularly carefully to any advice he is given.

Although there will be opportunities for the unattached Rooster to make new friends and find romance, it may be better to let any new relationship build up gradually rather that rush into any major commitment. By proceeding slowly, the association is likely to be put on a securer foundation.

While the Rooster may not have things all his own way over the year, he will still learn much from the year. As long as he sets about his activities in his usual careful way and is willing to adapt to changing situations, he can make steady progress. He will also be pleased with the work that he carries out on his home. However, 1996 is not a year for taking risks or ignoring the views and advice of others. If he remembers this, then the Rooster will do much to mitigate the more adverse aspects of the year. He will begin to notice a gradual upturn in his fortunes towards the end of the year and this upturn will gather pace as the next Chinese year, the Year of the Ox, approaches.

As far as the different types of Rooster are concerned, 1996 will be a significant year for the *Metal Rooster*. Over the year he should continue to set about his activities in his usual conscientious manner. If he is involved in academic matters, he will find his studies will be well-rewarded and will be worth the sacrifice in time and effort that he has to make. The Metal Rooster has many abilities and by adding to his skills and qualifications he will be sowing the seeds for his future success. In all his activities, however, he cannot afford to rush whatever he has to do or take undue risks. Progress will come from steady and applied effort. The Metal Rooster would also do well to remain mindful of the views of those around him, particularly his family and those in authority. Although he may not agree with all he is told, those around him do have his best interests at heart and speak with the benefit of experience. With the variable trends that exist for the Rooster in the Rat year, the Metal Rooster cannot afford to ignore and upset others unnecessarily. Too much of an intransigent attitude could bring him into conflict with those around him. Metal Roosters, take note! The Metal Rooster will, however, get much satisfaction from the travel that he undertakes over the year and from the time he devotes to his hobbies and interests. His social life will also give him pleasure, although he should try not to be too demanding of others. Sometimes, quite unintentionally, he tries to impose his ideas and plans on others, and this can lead to problems and resentment. The Metal Rooster also needs to watch his spending and should be wary of stretching his resources too far. Generally, this can be a satisfying year for him, provided he sets about his activities with care. The latter part of the year will be more favourable than the first part, with August and September likely to be happy and eventful months.

This will be a variable year for the *Water Rooster*. In 1996 he could find it difficult to accomplish as much as he would like and some of his plans may need to be altered. Admittedly, for one so active and organized, this can be a challenging and frustrating time. However, the Water Rooster can take heart. By being adaptable and adjusting to new situations as they arise, he can make positive gains. Indeed, in some cases he could find his altered plans will work better that his original ones and some of the events that happen over the year will turn out to be blessings in disguise. To make any sort of progress in 1996, however, the Water Rooster does need to be flexible in his outlook and, in cases of opposition, be conciliatory. This is just not a year when he can afford to go it alone or shut himself off from what is going on around him. Those Water Roosters in work will need to be particularly mindful of the views of their colleagues and if there are any matters concerning them, they would do well to discuss the matter openly rather than dealing with it single-handed. The Water Rooster will also need to deal with financial matters with care and would do well to check the details of any large financial transaction that he enters over the year. This is not a time for taking monetary risks or entering into speculative ventures. The Water Rooster's domestic life will keep him busy over the year and while he can look forward to some pleasing times with those around him, a family matter could cause him some concern. If problems do arise, he would do well to talk the matter over with those concerned rather than let it linger in the background. Throughout the year he will find that openness and rational discussion will do much to diffuse any problems. The Water Rooster will very much enjoy the travelling that he undertakes in 1996 and any holidays he is able to take will prove most beneficial for him. While events may not always go as well as he might have hoped, provided he is flexible in his outlook he can turn what could be a challenging year into a reasonably fulfilling and satisfying one. As always, much depends on his attitude.

The *Wood Rooster* is an achiever. He knows what he wants in life and works until he has obtained his objective. Such persistence serves him well. However, in 1996 he needs to pick his activities with care. He can make reasonable progress over the year, but this is not a time when he can be over-ambitious and commit himself to too many things all at the same time. Throughout the year he needs to maintain a strict sense of priorities and not stretch his energies too widely. Without a certain restraint on his part, he could easily involve himself in a lot but end up with little to show for his efforts. In his work the Wood Rooster will take on new challenges and while not all his tasks may go as smoothly as he would like, he can still make progress and impress others. There will also be opportunities for him to extend his skills over the year and those Wood Roosters seeking work or wanting to change their employment would do well to keep alert for ways in which they can widen their experience. Much of what the Wood Rooster does in 1996 will be rewarded in the following year, the Year of the Ox, which will be a much more favourable year for him. The Wood Rooster will also need to exercise care in financial matters during the year and would do well to avoid speculative matters or taking unnecessary financial risks. If he does enter into any large financial transaction, he should check the small print carefully and be aware of any implications he may be placed under. As with most things in 1996, he needs to proceed carefully and cautiously. He can, however, look forward to some happy and memorable times with his family and friends. His family life will be full of activity and he could be particularly proud of the achievements of someone close to him. Any encouragement and support that he feels able to give will be much appreciated. His social life will also give him much pleasure and during the year he will extend his circle of acquaintances quite considerably. It will, however, be a demanding year for him and it would be in his interests to make sure he allows himself time for his own interests and recreational pursuits. To drive himself relentlessly or not give himself the opportunity to properly unwind could leave him feeling stressed and below par and certainly not making the best of himself over the year. Generally, provided the Wood Rooster does not over-commit himself or take unnecessary risks, he can emerge from the year with some gains to his credit and be in a good position to benefit from the improved trends that will emerge in the latter part of 1996 and continue through 1997.

This will be a demanding year for the *Fire Rooster*. Despite his considerable talents he could find it difficult to make as much progress as he would like or to carry out all his plans. However, while 1996 will contain some frustrating times for him, provided he is prepared to adjust to new situations as they arise and look constructively at any problems that occur, he can still gain much from the year. If, in his activities, he meets with opposition from others, he should listen to their views and see whether a compromise or way round their opposition can be found. Or, if his ideas do not meet with the support he desires, he should try to strengthen them or see whether he can do better. Provided the Fire Rooster acts in a positive and constructive manner, he can make headway. However, throughout the Rat year, he cannot expect to have things all his own way or assume support will be immediately forthcoming! To make progress over the year will require considerable effort on his part. In his work the Fire Rooster needs to be careful, avoid taking unnecessary risks and at all times remain mindful of what is going on around him. This is not a year when he can act independently of others. Similarly, with financial matters, he needs to exercise care and restraint. It is also likely that during the year he could face some expenses connected with his accommodation and it would be in his interests to check all the costs involved. Throughout 1996 the Fire Rooster needs to be prudent in his spending and not stretch his resources too far. On a more positive note, he will find that a new interest he takes up will be most enjoyable, especially if it enables him to meet others and provides him with a complete change from his usual daytime activities. He can also look forward to attending several enjoyable social functions over the year, including a memorable family occasion. His family life will be active and while there will be many domestic matters that will require his attention and take his time, he will have some happy and enjoyable times with those around him. A younger relation in particular will be a great source of joy to him. Travel is also well aspected and some journeys the Fire Rooster goes on could prove most interesting. This may not be the smoothest of years for him, but with his alert and sharp mind he is well-equipped to face and surmount any difficulties that arise. In 1996 he will learn much about himself and will gain from the experiences of the year. The Fire Rooster's future is exciting and he has the potential to do well. In many ways, the Rat year will be preparing and strengthening him for the better and more prosperous times that lie ahead.

This will be a varied year for the *Earth Rooster*. In recent years he will have accomplished much, both personally and in his work. He will have learnt a considerable amount about himself and gained from his experiences, both good and bad. In 1996 he will be able to take stock of his present situation and think about his future. He should decide on his future objectives and if he feels he needs additional skills or qualifications he should take positive steps to obtain these. Anything constructive he can do over the year will repay him handsomely in the future. He would also do well to talk about his ideas and plans with others; he will be grateful for the support and feedback he obtains and the ideas he develops could have an important bearing on the next few years. In his work the Earth Rooster will make steady progress. Those Earth Roosters seeking work or wanting to widen their experience should follow up any opportunities that they see. By acting positively and constructively the Earth Rooster can make progress. However, in all that he does, he should be wary about acting without the advice or support of others. Throughout the year he needs to proceed carefully and remain mindful of other people. The Earth Rooster also needs to be careful in financial matters and exercise restraint in his spending. If he enters into any large transaction over the year, he needs to make sure he budgets accordingly and is aware of all the implications. The Earth Rooster's family life will be demanding and busy over the year and while he may despair of some of the pressures placed on him, his domestic life will nevertheless give him much satisfaction. Many Earth Roosters can also look forward to some splendid news connected with their family over the year. As this will be a busy year for the Earth Rooster, if he ever feels under too much strain or pressure, he should not hesitate to ask for assistance from others. He will find those around him most supportive and helpful – but the help will come only if he asks! He should also make sure he sets time aside for his own interests and recreational pursuits over the year; he will find these will be an important and valuable source of relaxation for him. The Earth Rooster will generally find the second half of the year more favourable than the first and this is also when he will make the greatest amount of progress.

# FAMOUS ROOSTERS

Kate Adie, Danny Baker, Dame Janet Baker, Severiano Ballesteros, Michael Bentine, Sir Dirk Bogarde, Barbara Taylor Bradford, Julian Bream, Richard Briers, Michael Caine, Jasper Carrott, Enrico Caruso, Charles Cazenove, Jean Chrétien, Eric Clapton, Joan Collins, Rita Coolidge, Dickie Davies, Steve Davis, Sasha Distel, the Duke of Edinburgh, Gloria Estefan, Nick Faldo, Bryan Ferry, Errol Flynn, Dawn French, Stephen Fry, Steffi Graf, Melanie Griffith, Jeremy Hanley, Richard Harris, Deborah Harry, Goldie Hawn, Katherine Hepburn, Michael Heseltine, Diane Keaton, Nancy Kerrigan, Dean Koontz, Bernhard Langer, D. H. Lawrence, Martyn Lewis, David Livingstone, Ken Livingstone, David McCallum, Jayne Mansfield, Steve Martin, James Mason, W. Somerset Maugham, Bette Middler, Van Morrison, Willie Nelson, Paul Nicholas, Barry Norman, Kim Novak, Yoko Ono, Donny Osmond, Dolly Parton, Michelle Pfeiffer, Roman Polanski, Priscilla Presley, Nancy Reagan, Joan Rivers, Bobby Robson, Paul Scofield, Sir Harry Secombe, Jenny Seagrove, George Segal, Carly Simon, Johann Strauss, Jayne Torvill, Sir Peter Ustinov, Richard Wagner, Neil Young.

| | |
|---|---|
| 10 FEBRUARY 1910 ∽ 29 JANUARY 1911 | *Metal Dog* |
| 28 JANUARY 1922 ∽ 15 FEBRUARY 1923 | *Water Dog* |
| 14 FEBRUARY 1934 ∽ 3 FEBRUARY 1935 | *Wood Dog* |
| 2 FEBRUARY 1946 ∽ 21 JANUARY 1947 | *Fire Dog* |
| 18 FEBRUARY 1958 ∽ 7 FEBRUARY 1959 | *Earth Dog* |
| 6 FEBRUARY 1970 ∽ 26 JANUARY 1971 | *Metal Dog* |
| 25 JANUARY 1982 ∽ 12 FEBRUARY 1983 | *Water Dog* |
| 10 FEBRUARY 1994 ∽ 30 JANUARY 1995 | *Wood Dog* |

# THE

# DOG

# THE PERSONALITY OF THE DOG

Everyone has his day and some days last longer than others.
— *Winston Churchill: a Dog*

The Dog is born under the signs of loyalty and anxiety. He usually holds very firm views and beliefs and is the champion of good causes. He hates any sort of injustice or unfair treatment and will do all in his power to help those less fortunate than himself. He has a strong sense of fair play and will be honourable and open in all his dealings.

The Dog is very direct and straightforward. He is never one to skirt round issues and speaks frankly and to the point. He can also be stubborn, but he is more than prepared to listen to the views of others and will try to be as fair as possible in coming to his decisions. He will readily give advice where it is needed and will be the first to offer assistance when things go wrong.

The Dog instils confidence wherever he goes and there are many who admire him for his integrity and resolute manner. He is a very good judge of character and he can often form an accurate impression of someone very shortly after meeting them. He is also very intuitive and can frequently sense how things are going to work out long in advance.

Despite his friendly and amiable manner, the Dog is not a big socializer. He dislikes having to attend large social functions or parties and much prefers a quiet meal with friends or a chat by the fire. The Dog is an excellent conversationalist and is often a marvellous raconteur of amusing stories and anecdotes. He is also quick-witted and his mind is always alert.

He can keep calm in a crisis and although he does have a temper, his outbursts tend to be short-lived. The Dog is loyal and trustworthy, but if he ever feels badly let down or rejected by someone, he will rarely forgive or forget.

The Dog usually has very set interests. He prefers to specialize and become an expert in a chosen area rather than dabble in a variety of different activities. He usually does well in jobs where he feels that he is being of service to others and is often suited to careers in the social services, the medical and legal professions and teaching. The Dog does, however, need to feel motivated in his work. He has to have a sense of purpose in the things that he does and if ever this is lacking he can quite often drift through life without ever achieving very much. Once he has the motivation, however, very little can prevent him from securing his objective.

Another characteristic of the Dog is his tendency to worry and to view things rather pessimistically. Quite often these worries are totally unnecessary and are of his own making. Although it may be difficult, worrying is a habit which the Dog should try to overcome.

The Dog is not materialistic or particularly bothered about accumulating great wealth. As long as he has the necessary money to support his family and to spend on the occasional luxury, he is more than happy. However, when he does have any spare money the Dog tends to be rather a spendthrift and does not always put his money to its best use. He is also not a very good speculator and would be advised to get professional advice before entering into any major long-term investment or commitment.

The Dog will rarely be short of admirers, but he is not

an easy person to live with. His moods are changeable and his standards high, but he will be loyal and protective to his partner and will do all in his power to provide her with a good and comfortable home. He can get on extremely well with those born under the signs of the Horse, Pig, Tiger and Monkey, and can also establish a sound and stable relationship with the Rat, Ox, Rabbit, Snake and another Dog, but will find the Dragon a bit too flamboyant for his liking. He will also find it difficult to understand the creative and imaginative Goat and is likely to be highly irritated by the candid Rooster.

The female Dog is renowned for her beauty. She has a warm and caring nature, although until she knows someone well she can be both secretive and very guarded. She is highly intelligent and despite her calm and tranquil appearance she can be extremely ambitious. She enjoys sport and other outdoor activities and has a happy knack of finding bargains in the most unlikely of places. She can also get rather impatient when things do not work out as she would like.

The Dog usually has a very good way with children and can be a loving and doting parent.

He will rarely be happier than when he is helping someone or doing something that will benefit others. Providing he can cure himself of his tendency to worry, he will lead a very full and active life – and in that life he will make many friends and do a tremendous amount of good.

# THE FIVE DIFFERENT TYPES OF DOG

In addition to the 12 signs of the Chinese zodiac, there are five elements and these have a strengthening or moderating influence on the sign. The effects of the five elements on the Dog are described below, together with the years in which the elements were exercising their influence. Therefore all Dogs born in 1910 and 1970 are Metal Dogs, those born in 1922 and 1982 are Water Dogs, and so on.

## Metal Dog: 1910, 1970

The Metal Dog is bold, confident and forthright, and sets about everything he does in a resolute and determined manner. He has a great belief in his abilities and has no hesitation about speaking his mind or devoting himself to some just cause. He can be rather serious at times and can get anxious and irritable when things are not going according to plan. He tends to have very specific interests and it would certainly help him to broaden his outlook and also become more involved in group activities. He is extremely loyal and faithful to his friends.

## Water Dog: 1922, 1982

The Water Dog has a very direct and outgoing personality. He is an excellent communicator and has little trouble in persuading others to fall in with his plans. He does, however, have a somewhat carefree nature and is not as disciplined or as thorough as he should be in certain matters. Neither does he keep as much control over his finances as he should, but he can be most generous to his family and friends and will make sure that they want for nothing. The Water Dog is usually very good with children and has a wide circle of friends.


## Wood Dog: 1934, 1994

This Dog is a hard and conscientious worker and will usually make a favourable impression wherever he goes. He is less independent than some of the other types of Dog and prefers to work in a group rather than on his own. He is popular, has a good sense of humour and takes a very keen interest in the activities of the various members of his family. He is often attracted to the finer things in life and can get much pleasure from collecting stamps, coins, pictures or antiques. He also prefers to live in the country rather than the town.


## Fire Dog: 1946

This Dog has a lively, outgoing personality and is able to establish friendships with remarkable ease. He is an honest and conscientious worker and likes to take an active part in all that is going on around him. He also likes to explore new ideas and providing he can get the necessary support and advice, he can often succeed where others have failed. He does, however, have a tendency to be stubborn. Providing he can overcome this, the Fire Dog can often achieve considerable fame and fortune.

## Earth Dog: 1898, 1958

The Earth Dog is very talented and astute. He is methodical and efficient and is capable of going far in his chosen profession. He tends to be rather quiet and reserved but has a very persuasive manner and usually secures his objectives without too much opposition. He is generous and kind and is always ready to lend a helping hand when it is needed. He is also held in very high esteem by his friends and colleagues and he is usually most dignified in his appearance.

# PROSPECTS FOR THE DOG IN 1996

The Chinese New Year starts on 19 February 1996. Until then, the old year, the Year of the Pig, is still making its presence felt.

The Year of the Pig (31 January 1995 to 18 February 1996) will have been a generally favourable year for the Dog and he should view what remains of it as a time of opportunity, a time of innovation and also a time for reflection.

In his work he can make steady progress and he should promote his ideas and skills as much as he can. The progress he makes and activities he undertakes will impress others and this will do much to further his prospects in the new year.

Socially, the last few months of the Pig year will be a pleasant and active time for the Dog. However, he would do well to involve others in his activities and be prepared to discuss his hopes and any anxieties he might have with those around him. Both his family and friends will be most supportive and will give him much useful advice and encouragement. He will be particularly grateful for the views of someone older than himself and he will find much reassurance in their words.

The Pig year will, however, have been a demanding year for the Dog and he should make sure he allows himself time for his own interests and gives himself the opportunity to unwind and have a break from his usual everyday concerns. If he is able to take up a new interest or hobby, especially in the weeks following the Christmas holidays, he will find that this will give him many hours of pleasure. In addition, a new interest could usefully add to his skills as well as lead to new friendships in 1996.

One area which could prove troublesome in the latter part of the Pig year, however, is travel. If the Dog is contemplating any lengthy journey at this time, he needs to plan it with care and leave plenty of time for any connections he has to make.

Generally, the Dog will have good reason to be satisfied with his accomplishments over the Pig year and by its close he will be well placed to make even greater headway in the next Chinese year.

The Year of the Rat starts on 19 February and will be a pleasing year for the Dog. In many areas of his life he can look forward to making progress and generally this will prove a most constructive year for him.

During the Rat year the Dog should set about his activities with vigour and be determined to make the most of his considerable talents. In his work he should promote his ideas, follow up any opportunities he sees and also use any chance he gets to widen his skills and experience. The early months of the Rat year, from March to May, could prove most significant for career matters. The Dog also needs to remain aware of the views and opinions of his colleagues as well as keep a close watch on all that is going on around him. This way he will be in a good position to learn of opportunities as they become available as well as being better able to win the support of others. Sometimes the Dog does have a tendency to withdraw into himself or keep his thoughts to himself and in 1996 he should try not to let this happen. This is a year of opportunity and he needs to be positive and assertive.

Any Dog who is currently dissatisfied in his present position or seeking work should actively follow up any openings that he sees as well as take advantage of any training schemes that he might be eligible for. For many Dogs, 1996 will be a year of positive change and one in which they will be successful in attaining a new and more satisfying type of work. The changes that the year will bring will in themselves give the Dog a greater incentive to do well, especially if he has felt he has drifted or been in a rut in recent years.

The Dog can also look forward to a considerable improvement in his financial position in 1996 and an investment he makes or savings scheme he starts could work out well for him. However, in all his financial under-takings, he should still be wary about entering into highly speculative ventures or taking on a large financial commit-ment without checking all the implications involved. For all his many qualities, when it comes to financial matters, the Dog can sometimes be a little too trusting and, without care, he could find his good faith misplaced. Provided he is careful, however, this can be a positive year for finance.

The Dog's domestic life will also go well for him and bring him much satisfaction. Those around him will be keen to advise and encourage him and throughout the year he should not hesitate to avail himself of their support. However, while he can look forward to many happy times with his family, a close relation could have a problem to overcome. In such a case the Dog should not hesitate to give what assistance he feels necessary. His views and sound common sense will be much appreciated and do much good, more than he may realize at the time. His social life too will give him considerable pleasure and he can look forward to some memorable and happy occasions with his friends. The summer months in particular will be an active time socially and for Dogs who are unattached, May to August could prove highly enjoyable. Throughout 1996 there will, however, be many excellent opportunities for the unattached Dog to strike up new friendships and romances. It is also a favourable year for the Dog to marry.

There will also be chances for the Dog to travel in 1996 – sometimes at short notice – and the journeys and holidays that he takes are likely to go well and be most beneficial for him. In addition, he will obtain much pleasure from his hobbies and interests over the year as well as being satisfied with any projects that he carries out around his home and garden.

However, in view of the active nature of the year, it is important that the Dog does not neglect his own well-being. He should make sure he eats a healthy and balanced diet, exercises well and gives himself the chance to regularly relax and unwind. This is particularly important if he is in a stressful or demanding occupation. To drive himself too hard without adequate rest could leave him feeling below par and not making the best of the year. Generally, however, the Dog will enjoy the Rat year and if he sets about his activities with determination and gives of his best, then he can make splendid progress. Also, if there is some ambition or objective that he wishes to obtain, he should work purposefully towards that objective. He can achieve much over the year and he will find that positive action on his part will lead to satisfying results. With the progress he will make, an upturn in financial matters and a pleasing domestic and social life, it will be a year the Dog will greatly enjoy.

As far as the different types of Dog are concerned, 1996 will be an important year for the *Metal Dog*. His personal and domestic life will be eventful and many Metal Dogs will have good reason for a celebration over the year. It is a time when the Metal Dog could get engaged, married, have an addition to his family or be successful in attaining a personal ambition. For many reasons, he will remember 1996 with satisfaction! His social life will, in particular, give him much pleasure and for the unattached Metal Dog there will be opportunities for romance and for making new friends. Socially, the summer months will be an especially busy and enjoyable time. The year will also bring about several changes. Some Metal Dogs will change their accommodation and, while this will take up much of their spare time, they will be delighted with how the move works out for them. Most Metal Dogs, irrespective of whether they move or not, will also spend much time over the year on DIY work and in carrying out alterations to their home and garden. This work will be most satisfying as well as doing much to enhance the property. There will also be significant changes in the Metal Dog's work over the year. Some Metal Dogs will obtain promotion and move to a more responsible position, while others will take on a completely different type of work. In both cases, the change at first may prove daunting, but the Metal Dog will rise to the challenge and acquit himself well. He has many talents and in 1996 he will be given every opportunity to demonstrate his true worth. If, during the year, he is able to add to his skills, he will find that this will do much to further his prospects in the future. This is a year which holds much promise for the Metal Dog and by setting about his activities in a diligent and determined manner, he will be delighted with the progress he will be able to make. Generally, this will be a most enjoyable and satisfying year for him.

This will be a pleasing year for the *Water Dog* and most of his activities will go well. His family and social life will both give him much pleasure and many Water Dogs will form new and meaningful friendships over the year. However, while the Water Dog is usually most considerate of others, he should pay particular attention to the views of his family members in 1996. They will offer him much useful support and advice, and while he may not always agree with all he is told, the Water Dog should remember that they do speak with his best interests at heart and often with the benefit of experience. The summer months will, however, be a most enjoyable time for the Water Dog and a holiday or break that he takes then will be most beneficial for him. He will also derive considerable satisfaction from his hobbies over the year and it may be worth his while to get in contact with those who share his interests, perhaps by joining a local society or club. This could make the interest that much more fulfilling for him as well as leading to some new friendships. Those Water Dogs in education will make pleasing progress and while sometimes they may feel resentful at the demands being placed on them, the work and study that they undertake now will prove of considerable value in years to come. The Water Dog will enjoy good fortune in money matters over the year; many Water Dogs can look forward to receiving a sum from an unexpected source. It could also be in the Water Dog's interests to enter any competition that catches his eye – several times during the year he will enjoy strokes of luck and success in a competition could be one of them! Generally, this will be a favourable year for the Water Dog and providing he sets about his activities in a positive and optimistic way as well as remaining mindful of the views of others, this will be a happy and constructive time for him.

This will be a fulfilling year for the *Wood Dog* and one which he will greatly enjoy. However, to get the most from the auspicious trends that prevail, he needs to have some idea of what he wants to accomplish over the year. Then, with some objective in mind, he can work purposefully towards achieving his goals. Without any such plan, he could all too easily drift through the year and miss some admirable opportunities. In all his activities, however, the Wood Dog will be assisted by the encouragement given by his family and friends and he would do well to discuss his ideas and plans with those around him. With a positive attitude and the support of others, he can make progress in almost any area of his life, whether it is his work, moving, taking up a new hobby or in some other way, but to get results, he does need to plan and take positive action. He will also enjoy success in financial matters this year. Many Wood Dogs will receive some money for work they carried out in the past or through the fruition of an investment. However, despite the financial good fortune he will enjoy, the Wood Dog would still do well to keep a watchful eye over his expenditure and avoid taking unnecessary risks. Provided he is careful, though, he will end the year in a much improved financial position. The Wood Dog will also enjoy any journeys and holidays that he takes in 1996, especially if they allow him to meet up with any friends or relations he has not seen for some time. If, in recent years, he has experienced sadness or felt lonely, he would do well to go out more and get in contact with others – socially, this can be a pleasing year for him and he can build up some good friendships as the year progresses. Generally, this will be a most satisfying year for the Wood Dog and by setting about his activities in a purposeful way, he will accomplish much. The months from May to August, in particular, will be a most favourable time.

This will be a significant and enjoyable year for the *Fire Dog*. Several changes will take place and, while some may not be of his choosing, the events of the year will open up new opportunities for him. In 1996 it is important for the Fire Dog to be flexible in his outlook and when changes do occur he should evaluate them carefully and see how he can turn them to his advantage. The Fire Dog has a most resourceful nature and out of the new situations that arise he can do remarkably well, particularly in his work. During the year the Fire Dog needs to keep alert to all that is going on around him and follow up any openings that he sees. However, one word of warning: many Fire Dogs do have a stubborn streak and to be intransigent or unduly stubborn over any matter could undermine their progress as well as impair their relations with those who matter. In 1996 the Fire Dog must bear this in mind. Those Fire Dogs seeking employment or promotion or wanting to change their work will find their determination and diligence rewarded, often at a time when they least expect it. Generally, this will be a positive and favourable year for work matters and the Fire Dog should promote both his talents and ideas as much as he can. In addition to doing well in his work, his financial situation will improve as the year progresses. He will also lead an enjoyable social life and can look forward to attending a variety of interesting social functions, especially in the second half of the year. His domestic life, too, will bring him much pleasure and he will be particularly proud of the success and progress enjoyed by a younger relation. However, in 1996, the Fire Dog does need to remain mindful of the views of those around him and be prepared to involve them in his activities. There is a risk that he could get so preoccupied in his own concerns that he does not pay as much attention to what is going on around him as he should. If he lets this happen, strains and tensions could arise and mar what will otherwise be an excellent year. If he can bear this in mind, his family life will bring him much contentment.

Generally, 1996 will be a successful and positive year for the Fire Dog and providing he is prepared to adapt to change and remain mindful of others, he will do well.

This will be a significant year for the *Earth Dog*. Almost as soon as the Rat year begins, he will be imbued with a greater confidence and feel more determined to make the most of his considerable abilities. And his energy and enthusiasm will pay off. Those around him will look favourably on his ideas and support him in his endeavours. In his work the Earth Dog will make great strides and should actively follow up any opportunities that he sees. Many Earth Dogs will be given greater responsibilities over the year or be successful in obtaining a better and more remunerative position. The months from March to June could be especially favourable for career matters. Also, if the Earth Dog is eligible for any training courses or can widen his skills in any way, he will find that this will do much to enhance his prospects. Positive and determined action on his part will bring excellent results. The Earth Dog would also do well to consider taking up a new skill or learning about a new subject over the year. Not only will he find this a satisfying and useful way to occupy some of his time, but also he could find the additional knowledge he gains will be of great value in years to come. The Earth Dog's domestic and social life will also give him much enjoyment and those around him will prove most supportive. If, however, he should have any matters that are worrying him or he feels under too much pressure, he would do well to speak of his concern to others. He will find the advice and support he is given will do much to reassure him and in some cases he could find he has been worrying unnecessarily. Generally, this will be an active, enjoyable and fulfilling year for the Earth Dog. He will feel positive in himself and with his many skills and abilities he is well-placed to benefit from the positive aspects of the year.

# FAMOUS DOGS

André Agassi, Kingsley Amis, Jane Asher, Brigitte Bardot, Dr Christiaan Barnard, Candice Bergman, Lionel Blair, Dr Boutros-Ghali, David Bowie, Kate Bush, Max Bygraves, King Carl Gustaf XVI of Sweden, Belinda Carlisle, José Carreras, Paul Cézanne, Cher, Sir Winston Churchill, Petula Clark, Bill Clinton, Leonard Cohen, Robin Cook, Henry Cooper, Jim Courier, Jacques Cousteau, Jamie Lee Curtis, Charles Dance, Christopher Dean, Claude Debussy, John Dunn, Blake Edwards, Sally Field, Robert Frost, Ava Gardner, Judy Garland, Bamber Gascoigne, George Gershwin, Lenny Henry, O. Henry, Patricia Hodge, Victor Hugo, Barry Humphries, Michael Jackson, Henry Kelly, Felicity Kendal, Sue Lawley, Maureen Lipman, Sophia Loren, Joanna Lumley, Shirley MacLaine, Patrick MacNee, Madonna, Norman Mailer, Winnie Mandela, Barry Manilow, Rik Mayall, Yitzhak Rabin, Golda Meir, Freddie Mercury, Hayley Mills, Liza Minnelli, David Niven, Gary Numan, Sydney Pollack, Elvis Presley, Anneka Rice, Wendy Richard, Malcolm Rifkind, George Robertson, Paul Robeson, Linda Ronstadt, Sade, Carl Sagan, Jennifer Saunders, Claudia Schiffer, Norman Schwarzkopf, Dr

Albert Schweitzer, Sylvester Stallone, Robert Louis Stevenson, Sharon Stone, Jack Straw, David Suchet, Donald Sutherland, Chris Tarrant, Mother Teresa, Ben Vereen, Voltaire, Timothy West, Mary Whitehouse, Prince William, Shelley Winters, Ian Woosnam.

30 JANUARY 1911 ∼ 17 FEBRUARY 1912     *Metal Pig*

16 FEBRUARY 1923 ∼ 4 FEBRUARY 1924     *Water Pig*

4 FEBRUARY 1935 ∼ 23 JANUARY 1936     *Wood Pig*

22 JANUARY 1947 ∼ 9 FEBRUARY 1948     *Fire Pig*

8 FEBRUARY 1959 ∼ 27 JANUARY 1960     *Earth Pig*

27 JANUARY 1971 ∼ 14 FEBRUARY 1972     *Metal Pig*

13 FEBRUARY 1983 ∼ 1 FEBRUARY 1984     *Water Pig*

31 JANUARY 1995 ∼ 18 FEBRUARY 1996     *Wood Pig*

# THE
# PIG

# THE PERSONALITY OF THE PIG

Life is a succession of lessons which must be lived to be understood.

*– Ralph Waldo Emerson: a Pig*

The Pig is born under the sign of honesty. He has a kind and understanding nature and is well-known for his abilities as a peace-maker. He hates any sort of discord or unpleasantness and will do all in his power to sort out differences of opinion or bring opposing factions together.

He is an excellent conversationalist and speaks truthfully and to the point. He dislikes any form of falsehood or hypocrisy and is a firm believer in justice and the maintenance of law and order. In spite of these beliefs, however, the Pig is reasonably tolerant and often prepared to forgive others for their wrongs. He rarely harbours grudges and is never vindictive.

The Pig is usually very popular. He enjoys other people's company and likes to be involved in joint or group activities. He will be a loyal member of any club or society and can be relied upon to lend a helping hand at functions. He is also an excellent fund-raiser for charities and is often a great supporter of humanitarian causes.

The Pig is a hard and conscientious worker and is particularly respected for his reliability and integrity. In his early years he will try his hand at several different jobs, but he is usually happiest where he feels that he is being of service to others. He will unselfishly give up his time for the common good and is highly valued by his colleagues and employers.

THE PIG

The Pig has a good sense of humour and invariably has a smile, joke or some whimsical remark at the ready. He loves to entertain and to please others, and there are many Pigs who have been attracted to careers in show business or who enjoy following the careers of famous stars and personalities.

There are, unfortunately, some who take advantage of the Pig's good nature and impose on his generosity. The Pig has great difficulty in saying 'no' and, although he may dislike being firm, it would be in his own interests to say occasionally, 'Enough is enough.' The Pig can also be rather naïve and gullible; however, if at any stage in his life he feels that he has been badly let down, he will make sure that it will never happen again and will try to become self-reliant. There are many Pigs who have become entrepreneurs or forged a successful career on their own after some early disappointment in life. And although the Pig tends to spend his money quite freely, he is usually very astute in financial matters and there are many Pigs who have become wealthy.

Another characteristic of the Pig is his ability to recover from set-backs reasonably quickly. His faith and his strength of character keep him going. If he thinks that there is a job he can do or has something that he wants to achieve, he will pursue it with a dogged determination. He can also be stubborn and, no matter how many may plead with him, once he has made his mind up he will rarely change his views.

Although the Pig may work hard, he also knows how to enjoy himself. He is a great pleasure-seeker and will quite happily spend his hard-earned money on a lavish holiday or an expensive meal – for the Pig is a connoisseur of good food and wine – or take part in a variety of recreational activities. He also enjoys small social gatherings and, if he is in company he likes, he can very easily become the life and soul of the party. He does, however, tend to become rather withdrawn at larger functions or when among strangers.

The Pig is also a creature of comfort and his home will usually be fitted with all the latest in luxury appliances. Where possible, he will prefer to live in the country rather than the town and will opt to have a big garden, for the Pig is usually a keen and successful gardener.

The Pig is very popular with the opposite sex and will often have numerous romances before he settles down. Once settled, however, he will be loyal and protective to his partner and he will find that he is especially well-suited to those born under the signs of the Goat, Rabbit, Dog and Tiger, and also to another Pig. Due to his affable and easy-going nature he can also establish a satisfactory relationship with all the remaining signs of the Chinese zodiac, with the exception of the Snake. The Snake tends to be wily, secretive and very guarded, and this can be intensely irritating to the honest and open-hearted Pig.

The female Pig will devote all her energies to the needs of her children and her partner. She will try to ensure that they want for nothing and their pleasure is very much her pleasure. Her home will either be very clean and orderly or hopelessly untidy. Strangely, there seems to be no in between with the Pig – they either love housework or detest it! The female Pig does, however, have considerable talents as an organizer and this, combined with her friendly and open manner, enables her to secure many of her objectives. She can also be a caring and conscientious parent and has very good taste in clothes.

The Pig is usually lucky in life and will rarely want for anything. Provided he does not let others take advantage of his good nature and is not afraid of asserting himself, he will go through life making friends, helping others and winning the admiration of many.

# THE FIVE DIFFERENT TYPES OF PIG

In addition to the 12 signs of the Chinese zodiac, there are five elements and these have a strengthening or moderating influence on the sign. The effects of the five elements on the Pig are described below, together with the years in which the elements were exercising their influence. Therefore all Pigs born in 1911 and 1971 are Metal Pigs, those born in 1923 and 1983 are Water Pigs, and so on.

## *Metal Pig: 1911, 1971*
The Metal Pig is more ambitious and determined than some of the other types of Pig. He is strong, energetic and likes to be involved in a wide variety of different activities. He is very open and forthright in his views, although he can be a little too trusting at times and has a tendency to accept things at face value. He has a good sense of humour and loves to attend parties and other social gatherings. He has a warm, outgoing nature and usually has a large circle of friends.

## Water Pig: 1923, 1983

The Water Pig has a heart of gold. He is generous and loyal and tries to remain on good terms with everyone. He will do his utmost to help others, but sadly there are some who will take advantage of his kind nature and he should, in his own interests, be a little more discriminating and be prepared to stand firm against anything that he does not like. Although he prefers the quieter things in life, he has a wide range of interests. He particularly enjoys outdoor pursuits and attending parties and social occasions. He is a hard and conscientious worker and invariably does well in his chosen profession. He is also gifted in the art of communication.

## Wood Pig: 1935, 1995

This Pig has a friendly, persuasive manner and is easily able to gain the confidence of others. He likes to be involved in all that is going on around him and can sometimes take on more responsibility than he can properly handle. He is loyal to his family and friends and he also derives much pleasure from helping those less fortunate than himself. The Wood Pig is usually an optimist and leads a very full, enjoyable and satisfying life. He also has a good sense of humour.

## Fire Pig: 1947

The Fire Pig is both energetic and adventurous and he sets about everything he does in a confident and resolute manner. He is very forthright in his views and does not mind taking risks in order to achieve his objectives. He can, however, get carried away by the excitement of the moment and ought to exercise more caution with some of the enterprises in which he gets involved. The Fire Pig is usually lucky in money matters and is well known for his generosity. He is also very caring towards the members of his family.

## Earth Pig: 1899, 1959

This Pig has a kindly nature. He is sensible and realistic and will go to great lengths in order to please his employers and to secure his aims and ambitions. He is an excellent organizer and is particularly astute in business and financial matters. He has a good sense of humour and a wide circle of friends. He also likes to lead an active social life, although he does sometimes have a tendency to eat and drink more than is good for him.

# PROSPECTS FOR THE PIG IN 1996

The Chinese New Year starts on 19 February. Until then, the old year, the Year of the Pig, is still making its presence felt.

The Year of the Pig (31 January 1995 to 18 February 1996) is an auspicious year for the Pig and the closing stages will be a busy and fortunate time for him. His family and social life will be most agreeable and he will be much in demand with those around him. He can look forward to attending some particularly enjoyable social functions towards the end of the year and will have every opportunity to add to his circle of friends and acquaintances. For Pigs seeking friends or those who are unattached, someone they meet in December or January could prove most important to them in the year ahead. The Pig will also have some pleasing times with his family and be particularly proud of the achievements of someone close to him. If he feels he can give any additional support or encouragement to any of his family members, he will find his efforts much appreciated and valued. Domestically and socially, the closing months of the year will bring him much joy and happiness.

The Pig can also look forward to some successes in his work at this time. Others will look favourably on his ideas and achievements and he could be given some additional and more rewarding responsibilities. Those Pigs seeking work would do well to remain alert for opportunities they can pursue. By remaining vigilant they could find their determination and persistence rewarded. Some Pigs seeking work could be successful in obtaining a temporary position which will not only add to their experience but could lead to a better position in the future.

Most Pigs will also enjoy some good financial news towards the end of the year, although the Pig could find the Christmas and New Year holidays more expensive than he initially envisaged. This could mean he will have to budget carefully in January.

Generally, though, the Pig can achieve much in the Pig year and in what remains of it he should aim to give of his best and make the most of the favourable trends that prevail.

The Year of the Rat starts on 19 February and is going to be a variable year for the Pig. He can consolidate any recent gains he has made and make a reasonable amount of progress, but it is not a year in which he can afford to take risks or trust his luck too far.

In his work the Pig will continue to impress and his astute business sense will be valued and appreciated. However, he will need to work closely with others over the year and make sure he has sufficient backing before commencing any new project. Most of those around him will be keen to support and encourage him, but he must not take this support for granted, nor adopt a too independent or go-it-alone attitude. Progress will come from close co-operation with others. The Pig should also be wary of taking unnecessary risks and if he does plan to make any changes in his work, whether in seeking promotion or switching to another type of work, he should find out what is expected of him before he agrees to any new commitment. This is very much a year when he needs to proceed carefully and cautiously. However, while the Rat year may contain moments of frustration and uncertainty, all the time the Pig will be adding to his experience and preparing himself for the better days that lie ahead for him, particularly in 1997.

The Rat year is, for the Pig, in many ways a year for consolidation, a year for taking stock and a year for planning. It is an ideal time for the Pig to think about his future and what he would like to accomplish. The ideas and thoughts he develops now could help him considerably over the next few years. The Pig would also do well to discuss his ideas with those around him – he will be grateful for the advice he receives, particularly that given by someone older and more experienced. There will be much wisdom in what he is told.

Those Pigs seeking work will, however, have several interesting opportunities to pursue in the Year of the Rat and if they are able to add to their skills by going on any training courses they will find this will do much to enhance their prospects. Similarly, all Pigs could find home study courses or evening classes especially satisfying as well as being a constructive use of their time.

The Pig will, however, need to exercise a certain care with financial matters over the year and would do well to keep a close watch over his level of expenditure. Without care, he could find his outgoings greater than he thought. If he should experience any financial problems, he would do well to take a close look at his financial situation and make any modifications he feels necessary. He could be pleasantly surprised at the difference a few alterations could make. The second half of the year will, however, be a much more favourable time for financial matters.

Domestic matters will generally go well for the Pig in 1996 and he can look forward to many enjoyable times with his family and those dear to him. He will also take much pleasure in carrying out jobs around his home and garden. While a DIY project he undertakes will take him longer and be more involved than he anticipated, he will be well satisfied with the finished result. Jobs of a practical nature will give him a great sense of achievement over the year.

The Pig's social life will be active and enjoyable and, for the unattached Pig, the prospects for meeting others and for romance remain excellent, particularly at the start of the year and during the summer months. Any Pig who feels lonely or would like more friends should make every effort to go out more and give himself the chance to meet others. Socially, this will be a most pleasing year.

The Pig will also enjoy the travelling that he undertakes and any Pig wishing to learn a foreign language, improve on his language skills or embark on some lengthy foreign travel could find this an ideal year to carry out his plans.

Providing the Pig proceeds carefully and cautiously over the year, it will be a reasonable one for him. In many of his activities he can make steady progress as well as gain much useful experience. Also, the work he undertakes and ideas he develops now will help prepare him for the advances he will make in the next few years, particularly in 1997, a much more favourable year for him. However, the Rat year will still contain many enjoyable times for the Pig, and his family, friends and travels will all give him considerable pleasure.

As far as the different type of Pigs are concerned, 1996 will prove both a valuable but challenging year for the *Metal Pig* – challenging because not all his plans will work out exactly as he would have liked, valuable because he will learn much about himself and gain from the experiences of the year. In all his activities the Metal Pig will need to proceed with care and caution. If he tries to be over-ambitious or to achieve his objectives without the proper preparation, he is likely to meet with disappointment and failure. If possible, he should set himself some objectives for the year and concentrate on these rather than spreading his energies too widely. In his work he impress others with his diligence and tenaciousness and, while he may not make as much progress as he would like, he will be preparing the ground for his future success as well as adding to his experience. Those Metal Pigs seeking work should again actively follow up any opportunities that they see and take advantage of any chances they get to add to their skills and thereby enhance their future prospects. The Metal Pig also needs to keep a watchful eye over his level of expenditure and, if possible, avoid stretching his resources too far. Although this will not be a bad year for him financially, it is still not a year in which he can take financial risks or involve himself in large financial transactions without budgeting accordingly. Domestically and socially, this will, however, be an enjoyable year for the Metal Pig and his family and close friends will give him much pleasure. Many Metal Pigs can also look forward to some personal good fortune – either by getting engaged, married or seeing an addition to their family. The Metal Pig will also thoroughly enjoy any travelling and holidays that he takes over the year. Even though he may not have things all his own way in 1996, it will still be a generally satisfying year for him and what he achieves now will help him considerably in the future. He should also remember that those around him want to see him succeed and should he have any uncertainties or doubts over the year he should not hesitate to seek their advice. His family, friends and colleagues will all be most helpful to him.

This will be an interesting and varied year for the *Water Pig*. During the course of it he will have to take several decisions regarding his future. This could involve changing his accommodation, a personal matter or, for the young Water Pig, changing his school or selecting some new area of study. In all cases, the Water Pig should not allow himself to be hurried or pressurized into making a decision or taking action against his better judgement. Time is on his side and while some of the choices he has to make may give him some anxiety, he will be pleased with his eventual decisions. He should, however, listen closely to those around him, particularly to his family. They do have his best interests at heart and often speak with the benefit of experience. Similarly, if he is troubled by any matter over the year, he should not hesitate to seek the advice of others rather than shoulder the worry by himself. He is in the fortunate position of having his family and many good friends he can turn to for advice. Also, if he involves himself in any large financial transaction over the year or has to complete any involved forms, he would do well to check the small print carefully and make sure he is fully aware of any obligations he might be placed under. With finance and bureaucratic matters, care and caution is needed. However, while 1996 will contain a few uncertainties, the events of the year will generally work out in the Water Pig's favour and give him peace of mind for the next few years. Those Water Pigs who move in 1996 will be well-satisfied with their new accommodation and a change in area could easily lead to new friendships and an opportunity to take up new interests. Both his social and domestic life will give the Water Pig much pleasure and he will be particularly proud of the achievement and successes enjoyed by a close relation. He will also enjoy any holidays or short breaks that he takes – he could find visits to places of local interest especially enjoyable. The summer months in particular will be a most fulfilling time for him.

In 1996 the *Wood Pig* needs to give some thought to what he wants to accomplish over the year and plan his activities carefully. If not, he could all too easily drift along and have little to show for his efforts. The year can hold considerable opportunity for him, but it rests with him to use his time wisely and constructively. With determination and his usual good sense, however, he can enjoy some worthwhile achievements in 1996. In his work he will do well and impress, although many Wood Pigs will see significant changes in the nature of their duties. Some may consider retiring, but the Wood Pig should not take any irrevocable decision until he is sure in his own mind it is right for him. Time is on his side and if he has any uncertainties he would do well to wait and discuss matters with others rather than take action he might later regret. Generally, the Wood Pig will find that over the year any uncertainties that do arise will have a habit of resolving themselves – and usually in his favour! He will have some truly enjoyable times with his family and friends in 1996 and many Wood Pigs will also have good reason for a personal celebration over the year, possibly because of the realization of a long-held ambition. The Wood Pig is also likely to be invited to several prestigious functions during the year. His hobbies, too, will give him much satisfaction and he might find it advantageous to get in contact with those who share his interests, perhaps by joining a local club or society. This could lead to new friendships as well as increasing the enjoyment of his hobby. He will find outdoor activities especially pleasurable and for those

Wood Pigs who are keen gardeners, walkers or enjoy being in the countryside, the year will hold many satisfying moments. There will also be several opportunities for the Wood Pig to travel in 1996 and the journeys and any holidays he takes are likely to be both interesting and beneficial for him.

This will be a mixed year for the *Fire Pig*. In some areas of his life he will find much happiness, but in others he could face delays and disappointment. In his work, in particular, he needs to proceed with some care. This is not a year in which he can take undue risks or commence new projects without first obtaining the support of others. Sometimes the Fire Pig can let his enthusiasm get the better of him and he will find that if he sets himself unrealistic targets or spreads his energies too widely, he could end up disappointed. In 1996 he needs to plan, stick with his priorities and concentrate on areas that he is most familiar with. His prospects will, however, improve noticeably in the last few months of the year and this is when he can expect to make the greatest amount of progress. In his work and general activities the Fire Pig also needs to remain mindful of the views of others and keep a close watch over his sometimes forthright nature. Those Fire Pigs seeking work or looking for a change in their present position will find their perseverance rewarded. They could be successful in obtaining a more challenging type of work and although at first this may prove daunting, it will give these Pigs a renewed incentive to do well and possibly uncover talents they never realized they possessed! This may not be the smoothest of years for the Fire Pig, but it holds much potential for him and what he learns and accomplishes now will serve him well in the future. The Fire Pig's domestic life will, however, give him much joy over the year and many Fire Pigs will be involved in a family celebration over the year – possibly involving a marriage in their family or birth of a grandchild. The Fire Pig's social life, too, will give him much pleasure and he can look forward to attending a number of interesting social events over the year.

This will be an important year for the *Earth Pig*. Several changes will take place which will cause him to reflect on his present position and consider what he would like to achieve in the future. In formulating his ideas, he will be much assisted by those around him and when changes do take place – no matter what area of his life they might concern – he would do well to take heed of the advice and opinions of others. Those around him do have his best interests at heart and he should remain mindful of their views. Some of the changes that occur in 1996 will concern his work. Many Earth Pigs will change the nature of their duties over the year and while these changes may at first give the Earth Pig some misgivings, he will rise to the challenges and win the admiration and respect of those around him. His progress in 1996 may not be swift – or entirely smooth – but he will impress others as well as broaden his experience. Those Earth Pigs seeking work should follow up any openings that they see and if possible extend their skills by undertaking additional training. They will find their persistence will be rewarded and that their accomplishments in 1996 will help to lay the foundations for better progress in the future, particularly in 1997. The Earth Pig's family life will be pleasurable but busy and he will have many demands on his time. However, while there may be moments when he will despair of all he has to do, those around him will be keen to support him and at busy times he should not hesitate to ask for assistance. This particularly applies to household chores! In view of the active nature of the year, the Earth Pig should also make sure that he allows himself adequate time for recreational activities and gives himself the opportunity to rest and unwind. He could find it beneficial to take up a new interest over the year and if he does not get much exercise during the day, activities such as walking, cycling or swimming will do much to improve his sense of well-being. Generally, if the Earth Pig uses his time constructively, this will be a fulfilling year for him and the ideas and plans that he draws up now will do much to assist his future progress as well as give him some worthwhile objectives to aim for. The Earth Pig has many talents and much going in his favour and by the end of the Rat year and throughout the Ox year he will begin to realize his true potential.

# FAMOUS PIGS

Russ Abbot, Bryan Adams, Woody Allen, Julie Andrews, Fred Astaire, Sir Richard Attenborough, Hector Berlioz, David Blunkett, Humphrey Bogart, John Bruton, James Cagney, Maria Callas, Dr George Carey, Richard Chamberlain, Jack Charlton, Hillary Clinton, Glenn Close, Brian Clough, Sir Noël Coward, Oliver Cromwell, Billy Crystal, the Dalai Lama, Bobby Davro, Robert Dole, Phil

Donahue, Richard Dreyfuss, Sheena Easton, Ralph Waldo Emerson, David Essex, Farrah Fawcett, Henry Ford, Emmylou Harris, Chesney Hawkes, William Randolph Hearst, Ernest Hemingway, Henry VIII, Alfred Hitchcock, King Hussein of Jordan, Elton John, C. G. Jung, Stephen King, Nastassja Kinski, Henry Kissinger, Kevin Kline, Hugh Laurie, Jerry Lee Lewis, John McEnroe, Marcel Marceau, Johnny Mathis, Montgomery of Alamein, Dudley Moore, Patrick Moore, John Mortimer, Wolfgang Amadeus Mozart, Marie Osmond, Camilla Parker Bowles, Michael Parkinson, Luciano Pavarotti, Shimon Peres, Lester Piggott, Prince Rainier of Monaco, Charlotte Rampling, Maurice Ravel, Dan Quayle, Ronald Reagan, Lee Remick, Ginger Rogers, Nick Ross, Salman Rushdie, Baroness Sue Ryder of Warsaw, Pete Sampras, Arantxa Sanchez, Carlos Santana, Arnold Schwarzenegger, Donald Sinden, Steven Spielberg, Emma Thompson, Topol, Tracey Ullman, Michael Winner, the Duchess of York.

# APPENDIX

———◆———

The relationship between the 12 animal signs – both on a personal level and business level – is an important aspect of Chinese horoscopes and in this Appendix the compatibility between the signs is shown in the two tables that follow. Also included are the names of the signs ruling the hours of the day and from this it is possible to find your ascendant and discover yet another aspect of your personality.

# PERSONAL RELATIONSHIPS

KEY
1 Excellent. Great rapport.
2 A successful relationship. Many interests in common.
3 Mutual respect and understanding. A good relationship.
4 Fair. Needs care and some willingness to compromise in order for the relationship to work.
5 Awkward. Possible difficulties in communication with few interests in common.
6 A clash of personalities. Very difficult.

| | Rat | Ox | Tiger | Rabbit | Dragon | Snake | Horse | Goat | Monkey | Rooster | Dog | Pig |
|---|---|---|---|---|---|---|---|---|---|---|---|---|
| Rat | 1 | | | | | | | | | | | |
| Ox | 1 | 3 | | | | | | | | | | |
| Tiger | 4 | 6 | 5 | | | | | | | | | |
| Rabbit | 5 | 2 | 3 | 3 | | | | | | | | |
| Dragon | 1 | 5 | 5 | 3 | 2 | | | | | | | |
| Snake | 3 | 1 | 6 | 2 | 1 | 5 | | | | | | |
| Horse | 6 | 5 | 1 | 4 | 3 | 4 | 2 | | | | | |
| Goat | 5 | 5 | 3 | 1 | 5 | 3 | 2 | 2 | | | | |
| Monkey | 1 | 3 | 5 | 3 | 1 | 3 | 5 | 3 | 1 | | | |
| Rooster | 4 | 1 | 4 | 6 | 2 | 1 | 3 | 4 | 5 | 5 | | |
| Dog | 3 | 4 | 1 | 3 | 6 | 3 | 2 | 5 | 3 | 5 | 2 | |
| Pig | 2 | 3 | 2 | 2 | 3 | 6 | 3 | 2 | 2 | 3 | 1 | 2 |

# BUSINESS RELATIONSHIPS

KEY
1 Excellent. Marvellous understanding and rapport.
2 Very good. Complement each other well.
3 A good working relationship and understanding can be developed.
4 Fair, but compromise and a common objective is often needed to make this relationship work.
5 Awkward. Unlikely to work, either through lack of trust, understanding or the competitiveness of the signs.
6 Mistrust. Difficult. To be avoided.

| | Rat | Ox | Tiger | Rabbit | Dragon | Snake | Horse | Goat | Monkey | Rooster | Dog | Pig |
|---|---|---|---|---|---|---|---|---|---|---|---|---|
| Rat | 2 | | | | | | | | | | | |
| Ox | 1 | 3 | | | | | | | | | | |
| Tiger | 3 | 6 | 5 | | | | | | | | | |
| Rabbit | 4 | 3 | 4 | 3 | | | | | | | | |
| Dragon | 1 | 4 | 3 | 4 | 3 | | | | | | | |
| Snake | 3 | 2 | 6 | 4 | 1 | 4 | | | | | | |
| Horse | 6 | 4 | 1 | 5 | 3 | 4 | 3 | | | | | |
| Goat | 4 | 5 | 3 | 1 | 4 | 3 | 3 | 2 | | | | |
| Monkey | 2 | 3 | 5 | 5 | 1 | 5 | 4 | 4 | 3 | | | |
| Rooster | 5 | 1 | 5 | 5 | 2 | 1 | 2 | 5 | 4 | 6 | | |
| Dog | 4 | 5 | 2 | 3 | 6 | 4 | 2 | 5 | 3 | 5 | 4 | |
| Pig | 3 | 3 | 2 | 2 | 3 | 5 | 4 | 2 | 3 | 4 | 3 | 3 |

# YOUR ASCENDANT

The ascendant has a very strong influence on your personality and, together with the information already given
about your sign and the effects of the element on your
sign, it will help you gain even greater insight into your
true personality according to Chinese horoscopes.

The hours of the day are named after the 12 animal
signs and the sign governing the time you were born is
your ascendant. To find your ascendant, look up the time
of your birth on the table below, bearing in mind any local
time differences in the place you were born.

| 11 p.m. | to | 1 a.m. | The hours of the Rat |
|---|---|---|---|
| 1 a.m. | to | 3 a.m. | The hours of the Ox |
| 3 a.m. | to | 5 a.m. | The hours of the Tiger |
| 5 a.m. | to | 7 a.m. | The hours of the Rabbit |
| 7 a.m. | to | 9 a.m. | The hours of the Dragon |
| 9 a.m. | to | 11 a.m. | The hours of the Snake |
| 11 a.m. | to | 1 p.m. | The hours of the Horse |
| 1 p.m. | to | 3 p.m. | The hours of the Goat |
| 3 p.m. | to | 5 p.m. | The hours of the Monkey |
| 5 p.m. | to | 7 p.m. | The hours of the Rooster |
| 7 p.m. | to | 9 p.m. | The hours of the Dog |
| 9 p.m. | to | 11 p.m. | The hours of the Pig |

RAT: The influence of the Rat as ascendant is likely to
make the sign more outgoing, sociable and also more
careful with money. A particularly beneficial influence for
those born under the sign of the Rabbit, Horse, Monkey
and Pig.

OX: The Ox as ascendant has a restraining, cautionary and steadying influence which many signs will benefit from. This ascendant also promotes self-confidence and will-power and is an especially good ascendant for those born under the signs of the Tiger, Rabbit and Goat.

TIGER: This ascendant is a dynamic and stirring influence which makes the sign more outgoing, more action-orientated and more impulsive. A generally favourable ascendant for the Ox, Tiger, Snake and Horse.

RABBIT: The Rabbit as ascendant has a moderating influence, making the sign more reflective, serene and discreet. A particularly beneficial influence for the Rat, Dragon, Monkey and Rooster.

DRAGON: The Dragon as ascendant gives strength, determination and an added ambition to the sign. A favourable influence for those born under the signs of the Rabbit, Goat, Monkey and Dog.

SNAKE: The Snake as ascendant can make the sign more reflective, more intuitive and more self-reliant. A good influence for the Tiger, Goat and Pig.

HORSE: The influence of the Horse will make the sign more adventurous, more daring and, on some occasions, more fickle. Generally a beneficial influence for the Rabbit, Snake, Dog and Pig.

GOAT: This ascendant will make the sign more tolerant, easy-going and receptive. The Goat could also impart some creative and artistic qualities to the sign. An especially good influence for the Ox, Dragon, Snake and Rooster.

MONKEY: The Monkey as ascendant is likely to impart a delicious sense of humour and fun to the sign. He will make the sign more enterprising and outgoing – a particularly good influence for the Rat, Ox, Snake and Goat.

ROOSTER: The Rooster as ascendant helps to give the sign a lively, outgoing and very methodical manner. Its influence will increase efficiency and is a good influence for the Ox, Tiger, Rabbit and Horse.

DOG: The Dog as ascendant makes the sign more reasonable and fair-minded as well as giving an added sense of loyalty. A very good ascendant for the Tiger, Dragon and Goat.

PIG: The influence of the Pig can make the sign more sociable, content and self-indulgent. It is also a caring influence and one which can make the sign want to help others. A good ascendant for the Dragon and Monkey.

# HOW TO GET THE BEST FROM THE YEAR

One of the chief values of Chinese horoscopes is that they help to identify trends for the forthcoming year. Once these trends have been identified, it is possible for each sign to know what areas of life are likely to proceed well and which could prove more troublesome. With this knowledge, the more favourably aspected areas can be concentrated on and care can be taken in those areas where the aspects are not so favourable. In this respect, Chinese horoscopes can serve as a useful guide.

Here, to supplement the earlier sections on the prospects for each of the signs, I have indicated how I believe each will fare in 1996 and how each can get the best from the year. The areas covered are: general prospects, finance, career prospects and relations with others.

## General Prospects

RAT: An excellent year ahead. The Rat has charm and ambition as well as a most resourceful nature and in 1996 he can put his talents to good use. It is a year for him to be bold and positive. With the right attitude, he can accomplish a great deal. A year of success and opportunities and one the Rat will very much enjoy.

OX: A good year ahead. The Ox can make pleasing progress in many of his activities but he must be prepared to adapt to changing situations. It is a favourable year to launch new projects and promote his ideas. Personally, the year will also bring him much happiness.

TIGER: This could be a tricky year for the Tiger. In all his activities he needs to act carefully and cautiously. This is not a year for taking undue risks and the Tiger would do well to keep a close watch on his rather impulsive nature. In 1996 he should plan and stick to the familiar.

RABBIT: A variable year. Progress is possible, although in all his activities the Rabbit will need to proceed carefully and avoid taking unnecessary risks. He may have to modify some of his plans over the year but he will gain much valuable experience.

DRAGON: A highly favourable year ahead. The Dragon should go after his goals and aspirations in a positive and purposeful way. With determination, he can accomplish much.

SNAKE: This will be a busy and generally positive year for the Snake. Throughout he must be prepared to adapt to changing circumstances and not be reticent about going after his aims and objectives. By being bold and assertive he can accomplish much.

HORSE: A time for caution and restraint. In 1996 the Horse should avoid taking unnecessary risks and should act closely with others rather than retaining too independent an attitude. He would do well to analyse his present situation and think about his future aims and aspirations. This is a year for learning and for planning. Much of what the Horse accomplishes in 1996 will help prepare him for the upturn in his fortunes towards the end of the Rat year and in 1997.

GOAT: This will be a positive year for the Goat. However, to obtain the best from it, he does need to plan and organize his activities well and resist the temptation of spreading his energies too widely. He can achieve much in most areas of his life, but to make progress he must be prepared to actively pursue the opportunities that the year will bring. For the enterprising Goat, the rewards of the year can be great indeed.

MONKEY: A splendid year ahead. The Monkey is blessed with a most resourceful nature and he will be given every opportunity in 1996 to use his talents to the fullest. It is a year of progress and enjoyment and all Monkeys should resolve to give of their best in this truly favourable year.

ROOSTER: This is a year for caution. The Rooster should avoid taking unnecessary risks and would do well to concentrate on specific matters rather than trying to spread his energies too widely. At all times he needs to remain mindful of the views of others and pay close attention to what is going on around him. If he encounters problems he would do better to be conciliatory and flexible in his outlook rather than remain intransigent.

DOG: A productive and enjoyable year. The Dog has many talents and in 1996 he should aim to give of his best. With a positive attitude he can accomplish much as well as having some most enjoyable times with those around him.

PIG: This is a year for the Pig to take stock of his present situation and give some thought to his future. The plans and ideas he develops, together with his accomplishments over the year, will help him considerably in the next few years. In 1996, however, the Pig would do well to avoid taking unnecessary risks and not take major action without much careful thought or obtaining the support of others. Although his progress may not be as swift as he may like, the year will still hold some pleasant times.

## Finance

RAT: A highly favourable year for financial matters. However, the Rat does need to be his prudent self and make sure he keeps some of his gains back for future years. This is a good year to invest and to save.

OX: An improvement in financial matters is indicated and the Ox would do well to consider investing or saving some of his money. He has good judgement in financial matters and will enjoy some monetary gains over the year.

TIGER: Considerable care is needed. The Tiger would do well to avoid taking unnecessary risks with his money and also watch his level of spending. This is a year for caution and restraint.

RABBIT: The Rabbit needs to be his usual careful self when dealing with money matters this year. It is not a time for financial risks.

DRAGON: A positive year for financial matters, although the Dragon would do well to consider saving or investing any spare money for his long-term future.

SNAKE: The Snake will be his usual shrewd self in dealing with financial matters and many Snakes will enjoy a noticeable improvement in their financial situation over the year.

HORSE: The Horse should avoid taking unnecessary risks with his money or spending out too lavishly. This is a year for caution and restraint.

GOAT: A good year for financial matters, but the Goat does need to exercise a certain caution in his spending. He can sometimes be too indulgent and generous with his money and, without care, he could quickly eat into any additional funds he may have.

MONKEY: A good year for money matters and, if possible, the Monkey should consider setting some money aside now for his long-term future. It could build into a worthwhile asset in years to come. He could also be successful in some purchases, both for his home and himself.

ROOSTER: In 1996 the Rooster will need to keep a close watch on his level of expenditure and should avoid taking unnecessary financial risks. Care is needed in money matters.

DOG: A successful year for financial matters, although it would still be in the Dog's interests to keep a watchful eye over his level of spending.

PIG: In 1996 the Pig does need to watch his level of outgoings, as they could be far greater than he thought. Although his financial situation will improve in the second half of the year, this is still not a time for getting involved in anything too risky.

## Career Prospects

RAT: This is a year of considerable progress and opportunity. The Rat should advance his ideas, start new projects and go after the opportunities that he sees. Over the year he can significantly improve on his present position, but he does need to remain both determined and persistent. The Rat is blessed with many abilities and talents – in 1996 he should make the most of them.

OX: Significant progress can be made and many Oxen will obtain a new and more rewarding position over the year. However, the Ox does need to show some flexibility in his attitude and take advantage of the opportunities that present themselves. He can do well in his career in 1996, but he does need to take the initiative. His ideas and talents will generally be well received.

TIGER: Modest progress is possible, but the Tiger would do well to concentrate on specific objectives and areas familiar to him. He should also try to curb his independent tendencies – he will fare better over the year by working closely with and involving others in his activities and plans. If he can widen his experience now, he will find it will help him considerably in the future.

RABBIT: The Rabbit can do well in work matters, but he does need to set about his activities with care and remain fully aware of the views and feelings of those around him. He should pursue any opportunities that he sees as well as take advantage of any chance to extend his skills.

DRAGON: Significant progress is possible. Through the year the Dragon should advance his ideas and pursue the opportunities that he sees. His enterprising and innovative approach will be well received over the year.

SNAKE: In work matters this is a year of change. The Snake can do well, but he needs to actively pursue his goals and aspirations. With his original and creative mind, he can accomplish much, but the initiative does rest with him.

HORSE: The Horse will gain much valuable experience over the year. However, in work matters he would do well to concentrate on specific objectives and think about his future aims and aspirations. The ideas he comes up with and work that he does now will prove most useful for him over the next few years.

GOAT: This can be a successful year for the Goat and by giving of his best and concentrating on specific objectives, he can make good progress. He should not be resistant to change and should pursue any opportunities he sees. The Goat can achieve much in 1996, but he does need to make the effort.

MONKEY: A year of considerable progress. Many Monkeys will be successful in obtaining a better and more responsible position over the year. The Monkey should actively pursue his aims and promote his ideas – in 1996 he will impress and come into his own.

ROOSTER: A year of modest progress. The Rooster's greatest gains will come from widening his experience and adding to his skills. Anything constructive he can do, whether going on courses, taking additional training or embarking on personal study, would be very much in his interests and do much to help his prospects. The next few years will be a positive time for him and what he accomplishes in 1996 will help to lay the foundations for the advances he is about to make.

DOG: A year of positive progress. In 1996 the Dog will impress others and his ideas will be well received. Many Dogs will be successful in obtaining a new position or will take on additional and more rewarding responsibilities.

PIG: Some progress is possible, but the main benefit from the year will be the experience the Pig gains. In 1996 he would do well to add to his skills and qualifications and go on any courses he can. Anything he can do to enhance his future prospects will be very much in his interests. The progress that he does make in 1996 will be the result of careful preparation and planning.

## Relations with Others

RAT: The Rat is one who very much values his relations with others and in 1996 his personal relationships will go well. Both his domestic and social life will bring him much pleasure and happiness and for the lonely or unattached Rat there will be opportunities for romance, to make new friends and generally to lead a much improved social life.

OX: In 1996 the Ox will be given much useful support and assistance by others and he should listen carefully to the views of those around him. Domestically and socially, he can look forward to some happy and memorable times and for the unattached Ox, this is a good year for romance and for making new friends.

TIGER: Domestically and socially, the Tiger's family and friends will bring him much happiness and support. If he has any worries or concerns he should not hesitate to seek the advice of those around him. Some new friendships he makes could prove significant in the future.

RABBIT: A year for care. The Rabbit should be wary about whom he lets into his confidence and not be misled by rumours or gossip. Also, despite the many demands on his time, he does need to actively involve himself in the interests of those around him, otherwise strains could occur. There will be romantic opportunities for the unattached.

DRAGON: An excellent year for both social and domestic matters. The Dragon's family and friends will be most supportive and he would do well to listen to the advice he is given. This is also a most auspicious year for romance.

SNAKE: Relations with those around him will go well and there will be many opportunities for the Snake to extend his circle of friends. For the unattached Snake, romance is well aspected.

HORSE: In 1996 the Horse needs to be mindful of the views and opinions of others and overcome his tendency to go it alone or act independently. Those around him will give him much useful support and advice – advice he would do well to listen to carefully. Domestically and socially, the year will contain some pleasant times.

GOAT: An enjoyable year ahead. The Goat values his relations with those around him and both socially and domestically the year will contain some happy and meaningful times. Those seeking romance or new friends will find much happiness in the Rat year.

MONKEY: The Monkey can look forward to some most enjoyable times with his family and friends. However, he does need to remain mindful of their views – sometimes his independent attitude and reliance on his own efforts can affect his progress and it would be a shame to let this happen in such a favourable year. This is, however, an excellent year for romance and for making new friends.

ROOSTER: The Rooster can look forward to some enjoyable times with his family and friends in 1996, but he does need to listen closely to their views and opinions and also keep that candid tongue of his in check!

DOG: An excellent year in which the Dog can look forward to having some enjoyable times with his family and friends. He should, however, remain mindful of any advice he is given by those close to him. A good year for romance and for making new friends.

PIG: Although the Rat year may bring some uncertainties for the Pig, he will be in fine form when it comes to his relations with others. Both his family and friends will give him much pleasure and domestically and socially this will be an active and enjoyable year.